A   SOMEWHAT

UPSIDE-DOWN

LIFE

ROGER SAWTELL

Acknowledgments.

Grateful thanks to all the people who helped to get this book written. Too many to name them all but the list includes Simon Villette, Claire Frost, Theo Sturge for computer help; Paul Dexter, Nancy Bell for proof reading and comments; Nigel Bell for genealogy; John Desborough, Matt Keen, and Margaret Williams for encouragement.

A Somewhat Upside-Down Life

APPENDICES:

ILLUSTRATIONS:

For Susan, wife, friend, helper, companion on
the journey, without whom much of what
follows would not have happened ..... with love

A   FOREWORD

Now in my ninetieth year, with limited energy and increasing forgetfulness, I asked a friend what could I do to make the world a better place. Was there some contribution I could still make, however small ? My friend said, '*share your values* '. So here is my life story, both the history and the values. The family tree indicates that no one in my parents' families since 1602 has lived to my age – so there is no time to lose !

In John's Gospel account of the feeding of the five thousand, Jesus says, '*Gather up the fragments left over so that nothing may be lost.*' (John 6:12 NRSV) The *fragments* filled twelve baskets. This is an early example of conserving the world's resources but also a message at a deeper level, that in God's world, every meeting, every conversation, every incident, every *fragment* of our lives is important and should be gathered, remembered, considered rather than thrown away. These are the building blocks of our lives together and so this memoir is a gathering of many *fragments.*

In her Backhouse lecture given in Australia in 1993 to The Religious Society of Friends (Quakers), Janey O'Shea writes :-

> '*In the topsy-turvy world of the way of God , as taught by Jesus, familiar categories turn upside-down, people with contagious diseases are touched and healed, a woman who prefers intellectual discussion to housework is highly valued, the unemployed get a day's wage for a few hours work, the good seats at a banquet go to the street people ... the charism of early Friends was their gift to live at home in the upside-down world of God's reign.*'

As I look back at my life, I recognise some *upside-down* elements. Susan and I have been involved in some unusual ways of working and living. For example, in material terms, my top earning years were in my late twenties and thirties and my salary got progressively lower as I got older. When I retired I was just earning the national minimum wage. When we married in 1957, we bought a six-bedroom house in Sheffield and have been down-sizing ever since. For over twenty years we were part of a shared 'community of households' when most of our contemporaries were becoming more independent. I became progressively less and less attached to any Christian denomination when most of our friends were more focused. We often seemed to be stretching the boundaries rather than conforming to the perceived culture of the time.

We travelled the world and I went swimming in numerous seas and oceans but very seldom visited any swimming pool until I was over 50. I have walked the hills of four continents but have never yet set foot on the highest point of the county where we have lived for nearly half a century. I was selected to represent the North of England at squash but never played for Yorkshire where we lived. All upside-down.

>*'O mortal , what is good; and what does the Lord require of you but to do justice, and to love kindness and to walk humbly with your God.'*

These words, from Micah 6:8 (NRSV), are deeply carved into a rugged oak bench which I made some years ago and installed at a remote spot at Pitsford Water Nature Reserve, near Northampton. As I look back I don't score many points for *walking humbly*. I blot out my shortcomings, and others see them more clearly than me, but I think I can claim some experience of *doing justice* , in particular the development of participative working practices in industry and commerce, with reference to employee-ownership and co-operative principles.

Ever since coming to Christian faith at the age of 20, I was searching for ways of living together and working together which might reflect Jesus' teaching, but it was not until I was in my fifties that practical projects emerged in the shape of Daily Bread Co-operative, at age 53, and the Neighbours Community at 57. Old enough to have learned a few lessons from life and young enough to have the energy to put them into practice. It is mostly what I have learned after spending over twenty years in both these organisations, that may be worth recording in these pages and passing on to others who may be interested.

There is almost nothing written by my grandparents and I wish they had left some record of their lives. My father, an orderly man, kept a careful account of our family life, especially holidays, but he was not a philosophical person and he seldom made any comment or drew any conclusions from the activities he recorded. In contrast, I have tried to show changing views, ethical concerns, emotional situations, value judgements, and a few anecdotes to balance the story of a varied life. This writing started as a contribution to family history but, when I learned that others were interested, I have revised it for a wider readership. If there is but one nugget of information or just one comment which may help to make the world a better place, then the the difficulty of remembering just what did happen, the toil of writing it down and the struggles with the computer, will all have been worthwhile.

Roger Sawtell   Northampton   December 2016

Horace (David) Sawtell – graduate apprentice at the railway works at Crewe. 1911 (aged 24)

Barbara Leslie, aged 15, with her father John Henry Leslie and two of her brothers.   London. 5 September 1906

Barbara Leslie,aged 20,when she and Dad first met. They were married at St.James' Piccadilly, London, June 1924.

Roger (5), Nancy(3), David (7). Alderley Edge 1932

Aged 10 at school at Arnold House, Llandulas. 1937

Dad and Nancy at the wedding of her friend Chinky.
London 1953

Bedford School 1944. Drawn by Bill Henderson.

B   DRAFT OBITUARY

A wise friend told me that everyone should write an obituary as old age approaches, in order to put one's life into perspective, so....

Roger Sawtell, who died on xxx aged xxx, led an unusual life at work and at home. He was a co-operative entrepreneur and also a founder member of a residential Christian community in Northampton where he and his wife, Susan, lived for many years.

Born in Sheffield in 1927, his parents sent him to school in Wales to avoid the bombing in World War II. From there he won a minor scholarship to Bedford School and then a State Bursary to Clare College, Cambridge, where he played a lot of cricket, made a handful of lifelong friends and finished with a 2:1 in the Mechanical Sciences Tripos. Without these scholarships his parents would have been hard put to it to pay the education bills. Susan Flint, daughter of a judge, whom he married in 1957, claimed he was brought up in 'genteel poverty'. Nevertheless it was a happy childhood with loving parents and always food on the table.

He served a two-year graduate apprenticeship with English Electric Ltd. at their Rugby works, the only place in the world where four prime movers, steam turbines, water turbines, gas turbines and marine diesels, were manufactured under the same roof. Wonderful experience for a young engineer, including having to manage the emergency shut-down of a 60 MW steam turbine after the night-shift supervisor had gone home sick. The managing director made a special visit to the site to congratulate him and his apprentice colleagues on saving the turbine from extensive damage, and offered him a job. However, he chose to look for a smaller enterprise and in 1950 was appointed assistant works engineer at Spear & Jackson Ltd., prestigious makers of tools and special steels in Sheffield, his home city.

The directors of Spear & Jackson, which had a world-wide market and reputation for quality, were proud to have developed the business over 200 years by 'sound Yorkshire common sense' rather than book learning and Roger was the first graduate they had deigned to employ. He soon became more interested in management than engineering, involving people at all levels in the decision-making process, as an alternative to the Spear

& Jackson tradition of benevolent paternalism. He became a Freeman of The Cutler's Company and a magistrate. In due course, ambitious and hard-working, his boardroom colleagues offered him the glittering prize of managing director, the post at which he had been aiming for most of his 16 years with the company. However, to his own surprise, and that of some of his friends, he turned it down and, influenced by the church's Industrial Mission to the steel industry, began to search for a more just structure than the conventional incorporated company, solely owned and controlled by outside shareholders. In 1967, with Susan and their four small children, the family made a 7,000 mile overland journey in a motor caravan to Israel where they stayed on a kibbutz and experienced the democratic structure of the community which included a small factory manufacturing tools from Spear & Jackson steel.

On returning to UK, aged 40, he met E F Schumacher, author of *Small is Beautiful* (Abacus 1973) and was deeply influenced by his philosophy. The course was set for the rest of his working life when he accepted an opportunity to develop a small employee-owned business making glassfibre canoes, Trylon Ltd. Thereafter he became an advisor to employee-owned co-operative businesses and drafted a set of Model Rules in 1976 for small co-operatives.   With a group of friends, he formed Daily Bread Co-operative in Northampton which started trading as suppliers of wholefoods in 1980. Both these small businesses continue to-day and he is probably the only person in UK to have initiated two successful employee-owned co-operatives.

In the 1970's he served as chair of Industrial Common Ownership Movement (ICOM), later amalgamated with Co-operativesUK, and also of Industrial Common Ownership Finance (ICOF), a revolving loan fund, the founding meeting of which in 1972 took place in the Sawtell's living room with their children running about in their pyjamas. This fund was the first community development fund (CDFI) and now trades as Co-operative & Community Finance, authorised and regulated by the Financial Conduct Authority (FCA). The Fund lent £1.4 million to co-operatives and other ethical businesses in 2014.

Following the financial crisis of 2008, the co-operative option became more widely known as a viable alternative business structure. Roger wrote a succession of articles and booklets about structures for employee-owned small businesses but claimed that his only best seller was a eucharistic 'bread and wine' Christian liturgy, *A Simple Communion - arranged for small groups,* which sold 10,000 copies and is widely used. This liturgy grew out of a house group attached to a parish church which turned into a residential Christian community in five adjacent terrace houses,The Neighbours Community, where Roger and Susan lived for 23 years. For part of this era he edited the magazine *Christian Community.* Darton Longman & Todd published his book *Under One Roof - the story of a Christian community* in 2015.

In the long history of The Religious Society of Friends (Quakers), he is thought to be the only non-Quaker to be invited to give The Swarthmore Lecture, together with Susan who had become a widely-respected Friend. This was published as *Reflections on a Long Marriage* (Quaker Books 2006)

A lifetime's familiarity with the four Gospels gradually brought him to the view that the church envisioned by Jesus was, essentially, small groups meeting round the supper table - agape. He put this into practice as an interdenominational Christian and also maintained links with Anglicans, Roman Catholics and Quakers, as well as the communities on Iona and at Taizé in France.

Always a keen games player, he played squash for Northamptonshire and continued to enjoy an occasional game with his grandchildren even when he was nearer 90 than 80. He was a hill-walker with experience in a dozen countries, and also also a strong swimmer having swum off the east and west shores of each of the three temperate oceans, Atlantic, Pacific and Indian, as well as numerous lakes and seas including the Med, the Red and the Dead. His nearest approach to the the Arctic ocean was a very brief dip in the icy waters of Puget Sound. In his 90th. year, he continued to swim 40 lengths (1km.) once or twice a week.

He did not live to see his vision of a large and significant co-operative sector of the economy become established but when his   inter-denominational prayers are answered, some may remember him as a contributor to 'a better way to work together'. He is survived by Susan, married for xxx years, four children and eight grandchildren.

June 2016

C   PARENTS AND GRANDPARENTS

I never knew my paternal grandfather as he died young of tuberculosis, leaving his wife, my grandmother, to bring up three children single-handed. To make a living she rented a villa at Hyères on the French Riviera and invited friends to spend the winter there as paying guests. This was quite a common practice between the two world wars. Her most distinguished guest was Mrs. Roosevelt, mother of Franklin D. Roosevelt, President of USA from 1932-1945. My father was sent to school at Epsom College and later found a place at Clare College, Cambridge, to study engineering. His mother could only afford two years at Clare, instead of the customary three, and although he seemed to have worked very hard, he failed his finals. However, he was then able to sit for an external degree at University of London, which he passed in 1911.* During his school and apprenticeship years, my father travelled to Villa Rossignols at Hyères for holidays and he claimed he had crossed the Channel over 100 times before he was 21.

*A generation onwards at Clare, I was fortunate not to be selected for a 'fast course' degree in Mechanical Sciences in two years, which,like my father, I would have certainly failed. I was able to do the full three years and get through satisfactorily.

Working in Sheffield at Cammells, a large engineering firm, my father volunteered in 1916 and went to France as an Inspector of Ordnance with the Royal Artillery, supervising the location of heavy guns behind the front line. As well as the standard war medals Lieutenant Sawtell was awarded the Belgian Croix de Guerre in 1918 for distinguished service during the final allied offensive which ended the war.
I think he was probably a conscientious and brave soldier but without the imagination to be a tactician or commander. He

once told me that the trait he admired most was physical bravery.

My brother, David, my sister, Nancy, and I were all born in Sheffield before the family moved to Cheshire in 1931. My father was appointed works manager of Richard Johnson and Nephew, a well-known family company in Manchester which , along with their deadly rivals, Rylands, dominated the UK wire-drawing industry between the wars. This was well-paid work and we lived in middle-class comfort with a live-in nanny called Olive, a cook (Whitey) who came in every day and a regular gardener, Gleave, who never divulged his Christian name. We called him 'Gleave', not 'Mr Gleave' which would have been more appropriate, and he must have considered us obnoxious brats.

Dad was the only senior manager who was not a member of the Johnson family but I had the impression that the Directors depended on him for his technical knowledge of the processes of wire manufacturing. He was very conscientious and aware of protocol, setting off to Manchester every morning in his bowler hat with a neatly rolled umbrella. I still have the hat.

In the mid-thirties he was the management negotiator during a long and bitter strike at Johnson's and when it was eventually settled, in no small manner by his efforts, the Directors sighed with relief and gave him notice, to make room for a young Johnson who had been his assistant. My father, a loyal servant, was devastated by the injustice of his dismissal and even for me, aged nine, it was an unforgettable experience that life is 'unfair'. He was unemployed for nearly a year, urgently seeking work at a level which would feed the family and pay the school fees for three children. From then onwards money was tight and our parents made huge sacrifices to send us to boarding schools. At that time, private education was not the social status mark which it has now become, but the only way that aspirational parents could get a good education for their children. When Susan arrived on the scene, her father being a successful barrister and later a judge, she reckoned we lived in 'genteel poverty'.

Granny Caroline retired to a cheap hotel in Bournemouth and spent the summer staying with friends, whether they liked it or not. She followed the strawberry crop from southern England in the early summer to Scotland in September, spending some time with us on the way. We children thought her a rather grumpy old person who doted on her son but took little interest in our mother or us children, so her visits were not the happiest times. On one occasion she had some kind of diarrhoea and left the bathroom rather smelly. I ran downstairs holding my nose and shouting 'poo poo'. Dad was furious, for his mother could do no wrong, and banished me to my room without any supper. He always called her Mater, was a very dutiful son and looked after her very conscientiously until she died in 1944.

In due course he found work as manager of the wire department at Samuel Fox, a large south Yorkshire steelworks, and we moved house to Sheffield. When petrol rationing was introduced, early in the wartime years, he applied for extra coupons to drive the ten miles to work, mentioning that he had often to be at work until late in the evening to keep in touch with the night shift. The civil servant in charge of issuing coupons replied that dad could catch a service bus to Stocksbridge every morning and gave him a half-ration to return home by car as there was no late evening bus. A classic civil service solution, seemingly rational but obviously not workable. So we moved again, renting one end of a farmhouse in Wortley, a village much nearer Fox's.

Petrol was scarce by then and he hid several large cans in an outhouse for emergencies. When he filled the car for some urgent journey he discovered, but too late, that a villain had discovered his hoard and substituted water for the petrol. It took many hours to clear it out of the fuel pipes and the engine spluttered complainingly.

My father worked long hours at Fox's throughout the war years and eventually retired in 1952 by which time he was manager of the various 'light departments' such as spring-making, tube drawing and wire production. Fox's decided to diversify and made some prototype steel-framed tennis rackets which were tested by professionals and seemed promising to the extent that Slazengers bought the production rights. They promptly decided not to continue the development as it would interfere with sales of their renowned wooden rackets, and it was many years before steel frames became commonplace for tennis and squash.   Undeterred, Fox's decided to enter the watch-spring market and sent dad to Switzerland several times where he was unsuccessful in persuading the Swiss watchmakers to buy their springs from Sheffield. However, Smith's, a significant but less exacting UK watchmaker, became a major customer and my father got the credit for this development and received a gold watch from them when he retired.

My mother was formerly Barbara Leslie, daughter of Colonel J. H. Leslie of the Royal Artillery. On retirement from the army grandfather Leslie worked in the steel industry and became a well-known public figure in Sheffield. He was a Freeman of the Cutlers Company (as I was fifty years later) and lived in some style, east of Sheffield. However, the money ran out by the time Barbara was growing up, the third of five children, and she suffered from painful feet all her life because she was not able to buy new shoes as a teenager. Grandfather was a highly respected historian of the Royal Artillery, a school governor and Scout commissioner. By the time we knew him, he was about 80, living alone in a bedsit surrounded by heavy historical tomes. My mother never encouraged us to visit him and I only learned later that she considered he was a bad influence on young people because the reason for the his impecunious condition was that he had spent large sums on 'chorus girls' who came and went at the Lyceum Theatre in Sheffield, of which he was a director.

Barbara, in her tight shoes, lived at home during the World War I and collected sphagnum moss on the extensive moors surrounding Sheffield, for dressing wounds in France. For many years she did the Daily Telegraph crossword every day. Her brother, Hubert, wrote to the paper claiming that he usually finished it in less than 15 minutes and the unbelieving paper thought to call his bluff by setting up a competition in London. The winner finished in 12 minutes and Hubert was second or third. My mother often finished it but worked by intuition rather than logic. She would say, " I think the answer is tiger but I can't think why." She was usually right and we children would be expected to explain it. I think she was a highly intelligent woman who had never had the opportunity of higher education because grandfather would have thought it was not necessary for a young woman, and anyway, he was short of money for reasons mentioned above.

My mother was loving and lovable and brought us up in difficult circumstances with total unconcern for her own interests. During the second world war, our three servants were all redirected to war work and mother had to learn to cook. My father who knew that she did not find this easy with rationing, scarcity, and not much money. He insisted we thank her often as well as thanking God for enough food to eat. My diary records the abbreviation AME nearly every day and , years later, I recollected that it stood for All Meals Excellent.

Her fine qualities were not always appreciated by dad and when she died in 1969 aged 77, he was surprised to receive so many messages of affection and appreciation, for he had tacitly assumed that he was the dominant partner. I think I may have fallen into this same error at times, by failing to appreciate what a strain for Susan were the uncertainties of my so-called career.   It was all very well for me to chase after new ways of organising work and enjoy the challenge, but we had four children to bring up and the main burden was on her rather than me. Our own children learned this lesson, or perhaps the culture had changed, and there is much more partnership now in family life. Our three sons-in-law are all good cooks and iron their own shirts – I can't do either.

D   CHILDHOOD - Alderley Edge, Cheshire

Despite the privations of dad's unemployment and then the war, my childhood at Alderley Edge was a happy time and I look back with thanksgiving and gratitude to my parents for making it so. Each of us had our strengths and weaknesses as children and, in general terms, they have continued throughout our adult lives. If anyone wanted artistic talent they would refer to my elder brother, David, who developed a gift for drawing and painting ; he had beautiful handwriting and a letter from him was also a work of art. But if they wanted something organised then they would come to me. "It won't be a muddle if Roger organises it", said my family so I suppose I was destined to be an administrator right from being a small boy. My younger sister, Nancy, with blond curls was everybody's favourite, of course, although David and I claimed she was spoilt for being the youngest and a girl. In fact, our parents showed no favouritism that I can recollect and gave each of us every educational and recreational opportunity possible within their limited means. Later, much later, we realised how much they had sacrificed on our behalf and encouraged them to travel at our expense before they were too old to enjoy it. They went twice to Africa as well as journeys closer to home.

My mother was an avid reader and taught us to read before we went to school. A few years before she died, her memory began to falter and she said she forgot most of what she read and was therefore happy to have just a handful of books, which she could read round and round. As well as the Bible, she enjoyed travel books and she shared in the family joke that "Mum is reading *'O'er Alp By Ox'* for the umteenth time." Dad was not a great reader; he kept a very dull book about Roman Britain in the car, to 'read in odd moments while waiting', but I do not think he ever read a single page of it. For at least ten years, on Sundays, he went to sleep after lunch, purporting to be reading H.A.L.Fisher's heavyweight, *A History of Europe.*

Summer holidays were very special and from 1934 when I was seven, until I left school at eighteen, we spent nearly every summer at Four Mile Bridge, a village which sits either side of the causeway across the tidal strait which separates Holy Island from Anglesey on the west coast of Wales. For many years this causeway carried the only road to Holyhead and thence to Ireland, so it is solidly built with a tunnel in the centre through which the tide surges twice a day. Long before we knew the area, an additional wider causeway, the Stanley Embankment, was constructed further north to carry the railway and the A5 trunk road to Holyhead, so Four Mile Bridge was by-passed and became a quiet village on the banks of a wonderful inland sea between the two causeways, ideal for sailing small boats.

We had a lovely 1930 blue Armstrong Siddely open tourer with a spare wheel on one running board and a large wooden box of tools and spare parts on the other. I still have have the box. My father used to remove the cylinder head every summer for de-coking and had an inspection pit dug into the floor of the garage. On one occasion, we removed the sump to access the main bearings and crankshaft and gingerly replaced the piston rings. This would have been my introduction to engineering and I enjoyed helping him.   Unhappily for practical mechanics, contemporary cars (2016) seldom need new piston rings and and getting at the engine is much more difficult because there are so many accessories under the bonnet.   Later dad swopped this car for an Armstrong saloon with a Wilson automatic gearbox.

A few years before the second world war dad also bought a Humber open tourer for £5 as a holiday car so that our 'ordinary' car, the rather sedate Armstrong saloon, would not get filled with sand. The Humber was an early version of what is now called a Sports Utility Vehicle (SUV) and in due course it did valiant work carrying sandbags at the time of the Blitz in 1940-41 before he sold it for £4.

In the 1930's, after school finished in July, the holiday convoy to Wales consisted of mum driving the Armstrong, full of children, followed by dad in the Humber, packed with sailing gear and sometimes pulling a trailer carrying our sailing dinghy, *Viking*. We used to stay for about four weeks and it was an unforgettable time. Dad came for his holiday fortnight and thereafter at weekends. There was no pub nor episcopal church in Four Mile Bridge so the village meeting place was the blacksmith's forge where Mr Parry had an ancient petrol pump. He pumped each gallon into a measuring glass in the body of the pump and then transferred it to the petrol tank of the car by winding a crank handle. It took about a quarter of an hour to put in the full eight gallons but I do not remember anyone suggesting that this was bad use of time. There was local news to be discussed and tide and wind to consider. Only later did we all try to do everything at breakneck speed.

We moored our little boat on the north side of the causeway because this was a good anchorage from which to explore the lagoon with its bays and inlets and islands, but if we were going south for a picnic at Cymyran or Silver Bay, we had to un-step the mast and take the boat through the tunnel. This was an exciting and sometimes hazardous venture because, at maximum flow, a huge volume of water filled the tunnel almost to the roof and the water speed would approach ten knots. Approaching the entrance, once the boat was caught by the current there was no way back. It was similar to shooting the rapids on a river but with the added hazard that if we misjudged the tide, there might be insufficient headroom, the boat would be smashed against the causeway and the crew might be decapitated. It was my first experience of the awesome power of nature and however calm the weather this immensely powerful force was at work, day in and day out. Volume is height multiplied by area and when we see the tide creeping slowly up a beach or inching imperceptibly up a harbour wall, the volume is not easy to comprehend because the area is so large. But when this same volume of water has to get through the tunnel in less than twelve hours it is impossible to ignore the power displayed. I have travelled all over the world since those childhood days at Four Mile Bridge but never seen a more impressive display of tidal power. At slack water when the tide was on the turn, it was quite different, we could swim through the tunnel and mess about in small boats catching shrimps and occasionally a lobster.

A handful of families used to go year after year to Four Mile Bridge for summer holidays and we renewed friendships with each other year by year. Regatta might be too big a word but sailing races were organised on the lagoon. These were agony for me because our flat-bottomed *Viking* would invariably limp in last with me in tears, seeing the well-designed boats, *Argo* and *Eros,* owned by more well-to-do families, go further and further ahead. The skipper of *Eros*, Mrs.Townrow was a formidable figure, clad in navy blue serge shorts and a seaman's sweater, barking orders from the stern. She was generous with her boats and, on one occasion, invited me to race with her and her children as crew. Huddled in our life jackets, sometimes sitting in the bilges to diminish wind resistance, we obeyed orders instantaneously and won the race.

First across the finishing line was greeted with a pistol shot from the starter, Dr.Townrow, a quiet man.   As a competitive boy I learned that decision-making by consensus, so important to me later in life as a manager in industry, was a hopeless technique for winning sailing races. One needed a clear-minded decisive skipper like Mrs.Townrow but, although I admired her competence and seamanship, I was frightened of her and glad to get back to our own unseaworthy mother who would be quietly sitting on the shore, knitting and making the picnic lunch.

Sometimes the village cobbler, Sam Jones, would take the helm. He knew every corner of the inland sea and while visitors invariably went aground, Sam would glide over the rocks and shoals to be first across the line. He had a wooden leg and belayed the jib sheet to it so, by moving his knee a small amount, he gained a fine control over the setting of the jib which enabled him to edge ahead of the fleet. To see these well-designed clinker-built boats go to windward while we, in *Viking,* slid inevitably on to the lee shore, was another lesson to me. The amazing forces of nature, in this case wind, can be used to advantage but only by studying the dynamics with the greatest care is it possible to sail north in a northerly wind. *Eros* could do it, *Viking* could not.   I pondered this in tears while pushing *Viking* off yet another sandbank and decided to be an engineer when I grew up.

When our family finances improved a little, dad ordered a brand new boat from the top-quality boat-builder at Beaumaris, with a view to improving our disastrous sailing performance. A price was agreed and the boat was to be built during the winter. Dad, sitting by the fire at home, enjoyed thinking of refinements to be added to this, the first boat he had ever commissioned. The dagger plate should surely have a curved leading edge; the cleats should be brass rather than zinc-plated steel; a pennant at the masthead would be nice. With sketches and explanations these refinements were posted to the boat-builder but, ominously, he did not reply. Being a man of impeccable financial rectitude, dad assumed he would pay for these additions but apparently had not made this clear so the boat-builder thought that he was expected to provide these extras within the quoted price. Dad's Christmas break provided time for a few more refinements to be sent to the boatyard but in January the original order was returned by post, with no comment but the one word CANCELLED scrawled across it in red ink. Shocked and disappointed, I envisaged another humiliating sailing season ahead. From this I learned another early lesson which stayed with me throughout my working life as an administrator - confirm decisions in writing, when making arrangements between groups with different priorities.

We also had swimming races. Our friend George Naish owned a half-decked boat and one day he took on board a group of us holiday children, moored his boat offshore and lined us up on the starboard deck, ready to dive in and race to the shore where our parents were waiting, pleased that winter swimming lessons were put to good use. George, standing on the port deck, fired his starting pistol, we all leaped into the sea , the boat rolled back and George was catapulted backwards into the water, fully clothed and clutching his pistol. We were unaware of his predicament as we swam for the shore, but surprised that, rather than admiring our swimming, the adults were convulsed with laughter at George extracting himself from the muddy water, swearing loudly. I can't remember if he lost his pistol.

Dad did not appear to be an imaginative man but in 1937 he had just one very imaginative idea. He obtained several hundred brass 'coins' which banks used as counter weights for weighing cash deposits. They had a king's head stamped on them and looked like gold but were of almost no value. Together with worthless glass 'jewels' from Woolworths, he sewed them into small leather pouches which mum ran-up on her sewing machine. He put them into a wooden chest with rope handles and a rusty lock and, with the help of other adult conspirators, buried it in the sand near Pork Pie island about a mile south of Four Mile Bridge, below the high tide mark so that all traces were obliterated. The following morning he came down to breakfast waving a parchment map which he said he had found in a drawer. It showed that mutineers from *HMS Temeraire* in 1850 had buried some stolen treasure near Pork Pie island. So, amid great excitement, a large party of children set off with the parchment and bamboo beanpoles for detecting hard objects under the sand. After taking bearings and sucking pencils and much prodding with the beanpoles, a hard object was indeed located and furious digging uncovered the box, four feet down, with *HMS Temeraire* painted in red on the lid. The treasure hoard was examined with awe and the chest carried home in triumph. We used the brass counters for years for board games and the chest for shoe-cleaning materials until it fell apart, fifty years later. It was a wonderful day but, aged ten, I was in some doubt for a year or two about what was real and what was subterfuge. A bit like Father Christmas or Harry Potter ?

We were a happy family with loving parents. Holidays at Four Mile Bridge were a highlight of the year and, as indicated above, they were also an important part of our education. When he retired from his work as an architect, my brother David returned there many times, messing about in small boats and recreating the past.

E   ARNOLD HOUSE,LLANDDULAS.1935-1941 (aged 8-14)

' R.D.Sawtell   September 1935 - Lent 1941
House: Pipons   ViceCaptain: Autumn 1940
                              Captain: Lent 1941
Prefect: Autumn 1940
Head of School: Lent 1941
Rugger XV: Colours
Cricket XI : Colours 1939   Vice-Captain 1940
Soccer XI: Colours 1940
Public School : Bedford
Cups: Worswick Memorial: Autumn 1936 and Summer 1937 '

These pretentious words are inscribed on the title page of a hardback *Merchant of Venice,* presumably given to me on leaving Arnold House, an extraordinary boarding school at Llanddulas, on the coast of North Wales.   The school was recommended to my parents because the Bishop of Chester, Geoffrey Fisher, subsequently Archbishop of Canterbury, sent some of his numerous sons there.   I recollect that one of them G.R.C.Fisher (Bobby), played Portia to great acclaim in the school production, kitted out in a floor length blue velvet gown. It all seemed rather odd, but we spouted Shakespeare's lines without having much idea of their meaning.   In the 1939 production of *Richard II* I had been Aumerle and this must have been the peak of my acting career, aged 12, because the following year I was downgraded to be some kind of spear carrier in *Merchant.*   I then 'rested' for over forty years before being persuaded to be First Tempter in a church production of *Murder in the Cathedral* in Northampton :-

' Here I have come, forgetting all acrimony, hoping that your present gravity will find excuse for my humble levity...... '

I had some difficulty in remembering these lines and have continued to rest from the stage ever since.

I remember playing a lot of cricket at Arnold House but have little memory of 'rugger' or 'soccer'. Maybe the headmaster made it up to please my parents. I have no recollection of being Head of School in 1941, but I do remember that the school motto was *Laborare est Orare*. I think we laboured rather more than we prayed. The Worswick Memorial Cup was for 'all round excellence' and I note that my excellence seems to have faded away after the first two years.

In retrospect, it may have been less the quality of the school that gained the patronage of the Bishop of Chester and more the fact that Llanddulas was only 30 miles down the main line from Manchester, near where we lived. In the uneasy late thirties and subsequent outbreak of war in 1939, it was practical to have children in a safe area away from bombing but within easy access. From the school grounds we saw Liverpool on fire during the air raids in 1940.

I doubt also that the Bishop was aware that Evelyn Waugh had been on the staff for a short time in the 1920's and had found it so dispiriting that he decided to drown himself by swimming out to sea from the bleak pebble beach at Llanddulas. However, the sea was very cold and he changed his mind and swam back again,later writing *Put Out More Flags* , a novel about a hideous prep school which must have been based on his own experience at Arnold House.

Following my brother, David, I was at this extraordinary school for nearly six years from age eight to fourteen. Although I enjoyed most of my time there and made some good friends,

I was also dreadfully homesick at the beginning of each term and vowed never to send to boarding school any children I might have.   Susan's boarding school experience had been similarly unsatisfactory and we never did.

The owner and head master of Arnold House in my first few years there was R.W.Fitz-Aucher.   On Sunday evenings the senior boys were allowed to sit on the floor in his study and read old volumes of Punch. I recollect this conversation :-

Fitz-Aucher: *"Come over here, Mudford, I want to talk to you."*
Mudford (who feared no foe) : *"No I won't, Sir."*
Fitz -Aucher: *"Why not?"*
Mudford: *" Because I know that all you want to do is to put your hand up my trousers."*

We had no other experience to compare this with so assumed it was normal behaviour. When a friend tried to talk to his mother about such practices she said, tartly. *"Henry, we don't talk about things like that."* It remained a great mystery.

Mudford also starred in the cheese waffle incident. Our latin teacher was a strict disciplinarian and sometimes we were unjustly punished so Mudford planned a revenge. Purporting to be the school caterer he ordered by telephone a large quantity of cheese waffles to be delivered at a specific time to Mr. Banks.   There was a knock on the classroom door and the caretaker came in to say that there was a delivery for Mr Banks.
"Oh yes", said Mr Banks, *"it will be the new Latin primers."*
"The delivery man wants paying for it," said Gwylym.
" Tell him to put it on the school account," said Mr Banks.
" He won't do that, Mr Banks, and he won't let go of the

*carton until he's got his money. Twenty three pounds and
sixpence."*

" *Very well then,"* said Mr Banks, reluctantly taking out his
wallet. Gwylym soon returned bearing a huge box.

" *Oh sir,"* said Mudford innocently, *"Do let's open it so that we
can use the new Latin primers you have so kindly got for us."*

Mr Banks opened the carton and exploded with rage as
greasy lukewarm cheese waffles spilled out all over his desk.

"Oh sir," said Mudford, *"I think we had better eat them
before they go cold."*

Mudford and his friend Sandham were always on the look out
for abnormalities in our teachers. Mr Wood told us he had
visited South Africa. He was in the habit of scratching his
backside as he addressed the class and Mudford and Sandham
spread the story, without any foundation whatsoever, that he
was a diamond smuggler and used to swallow the diamonds to
get through customs. One had got stuck in his bowels and that
was why he was scratching all the time. We believed this
story.

There was a wonderful younger teacher, R.C.Peile who inspired
us to be interested in English literature and I have reason to
be grateful to him ever since for a continuing interest in the
reading and writing of books. Peile was called-up and we heard
a year later that he had been killed in action. I could not see
the sense of war as a civilised way to settle differences and
later became a near-pacifist.

Fitz-Aucher was a good cricketer. He coached us assiduously
and arranged matches with other schools. The high-spot of
the season was a 'staff & boys' fixture with Woodlands, a
school a few miles away. I was wicket-keeper, a specialist role

and needed for this crucial match as there were not enough staff to complete the team.   The opening batsman for their side was a Mr Angelo, or some such name, who was their newly-appointed cricket coach and rumoured to be a 'professional cricketer'.   He was out, caught behind the wicket, and I was showered with praise by Fitz-Aucher and the other teachers. I wondered why, because it was not a particularly difficult catch. I did not realise how much prestige hung on this match. However, disaster ensued as Angelo turned out to be a fast bowler and dismissed us with little trouble, winning the match for Woodlands. Fitz-Aucher vowed to be revenged .

Half way through the summer term the following year, two new teachers appeared, Frank Fisher and Maurice Pyman, both good cricketers.   With their help, Woodlands were soundly defeated and Fitz-Aucher was delighted , but we never saw Fisher and Pyman again. A few years later I happened to meet Frank Fisher, who was another of the Archbishop's sons, and he told me that Fitz-Aucher had engaged him and Pyman, both Cambridge cricket Blues, to join the staff for a few weeks after their university term had ended, in order to play in this crucial match. The fee-paying parents would not have been aware of these happenings. Although they did little or no teaching during their brief stay at Arnold House, Frank Fisher must have liked the role as he subsequently spent his life as a teacher, and in due course, was Headmaster of Wellington College or some such prestigious school.

When we returned to school for the autumn term 1940, Fitz-Aucher's Rolls Royce, with a fitted cocktail cabinet in the back, was missing and we learned he was in prison for some financial property fraud.   We realised later that he was an imposter as well as a paedophile, which was probably not uncommon among owners of private schools at that time.

Another feature we did not know at the time was that these preparatory schools were bought and sold as going concerns, without any particular reference to the standard of education provided. Arnold House was amalgamated with another local school, called Heronwater. Keith Gaskell was headmaster, a less colourful character than Fitz-Aucher but probably a more responsible owner.

Despite these strange happenings, of which our parents were hardly aware, and despite my continuing homesickness at the beginning of each term, I recollect enjoying my years there and I must have learned something as I was awarded a minor scholarship to Bedford School. Without this my parents would have been significantly impoverished, as David was still at Marlborough College and Nancy would soon go to The Abbey at Malvern, so they were paying boarding fees for all three of us.

F   BEDFORD SCHOOL 1941-1945   (14-18)

I was a boarder at Bedford School throughout the last four years of the second world war and travelled by train many times to Bedford from our home in Sheffield. The station names were 'blacked-out' or very dimly lit, to deter the potential German invaders from knowing where they were and industrial areas like Sheffield were also blacked-out to hide them from German bombers. Travelling was difficult and not encouraged. Government posters asked *Is Your Journey REALLY Necessary?*   Clearly, my parents were undeterred and considered my journey to Bedford was really necessary. From Arnold House I had seen Liverpool in flames on the horizon and Sheffield was seriously bombed in my absence at school. Although Bedford was much nearer London it was not a target but one night a lost German Dornier droned overhead and dropped one superfluous bomb on the town. Next day we went eagerly to see the bomb crater, twenty foot deep, and redoubled the fire-watching rota on the roof of the Great Hall at the school every night.

My cousin, Dick Shuttleworth, a dashing young man and a hero for me, trained as a fighter pilot and was shot down and killed over France. A boy at my boarding house, a year or two older than me, was called-up and died when an ammunition ship blew-up in the Mediterranean. We kept silence in memory of Fowler at morning assembly.   I struggle to-day with computer technology and our grandchildren help me out with patience and effortless competence, but I know, and they don't, how to put out an incendiary bomb with a tin bucket. I pray they will never need to learn such knowledge from me or anyone else. You do not pour water on the bomb but smother it with sand.

We did our fire-watching and were marched about the grounds in uniform but these wartime experiences were not onerous and for most of the time the war seemed to have surprisingly little impact on school life, possibly because we had known no other conditions.

In the summer holidays we went from school to Ledbury, near Malvern, to a farming camp, helping to get the harvest in and picking fruit for the local canning factory. I earned nineteen shillings and three pence, about 90p, for a week's work and was proud of my first wages. One day after work I cycled to Malvern with a friend to visit my sister, Nancy, who was still at school there. In our farming clothes and unwashed state, I rang the front door bell of the head mistress' house and Miss Evershed came to the door. She did not accept that anyone so disreputable could possibly have a sister at her school and sent us packing.

A disappointment for me at Bedford was when a special Guard of Honour was chosen for a formal visit by the Duchess of Gloucester and I was not tall enough to qualify. I remained well under average height until I was about seventeen after which I finished at comfortably over six foot. Size did not seem to affect my enjoyment of all manner of games including tennis and golf at home and at school, cricket in the summer and Rugby Fives in the winter. The team photos show me usually sitting cross-legged on the ground while the leading players occupied the front row seats, with their arms crossed.

I was a natural schoolboy, finding the book work undemanding and the rules satisfactory. Only much later did I become a rebel and a radical reformer in industry. Inevitably at Bedford I was called upon to take office as a Monitor or an

NCO in the army corps and was strangely appointed Head of the Chapel Choir for a term even though I could hardly read music. A single letter home survives from 1944 when I was seventeen :-

> *' I have got a post of authority this term, which is rather annoying as I shall have plenty to do what with cricket and work. I have been appointed Head of the Barn which means I am in charge of most of the House... organising the fagging etc. I have to see that everyone behaves themselves and beat the little boys when they are naughty. PS This is a terrible job. People coming and asking stupid questions all day. Very annoying. '*

I must have been a horribly supercilious school boy, but perhaps most of us were the same because I had lots of friends. Barbaric corporal punishment we took for granted. As new boys, for small misdemeanours, we were bent over the back of a chair and beaten with a three-foot cane by prefects only a year or two older than ourselves, and when my turn came, I have no recollection of questioning the necessity for this aggressive regime. At morning assembly in the Great Hall with 500 boys present, the Monitors stood in the aisles with long canes held at the ready, and gave a crack on the head to any boy seen talking or sucking sweets or committing any other heinous crime. The most respected Monitors were those who could creep along the row behind and mete out this punishment without the culprit realising that he had been spotted. To-day, parents would be knocking on the Headmaster's door and threatening court action for assault. Quite right too.

There was no drug culture at school nor do I recollect any alcohol or binge drinking problems but sex was of interest to us, as I suppose it has been for teenage boys from time immemorial. Some of the prefects claimed to have girl friends at Bedford High School for Girls but sometimes this was illusory or 'virtual' rather than factual. During my last year I was approached by a small boy who said his sister was the wicket-keeper for the Girls School cricket team and would like to meet me as her opposite number. We met just once, at Lyons teashop which was the accepted trysting place in the town, but nothing came of it and I reckoned cricket was more important than romance. It was not till I got to university that I met anyone who had had an actual sexual relationship with a girl and it remained something of a mystery to me.

We knew a little about the facts of life but our knowledge was incomplete. In the Christmas holidays, boys were employed to deliver the post. The rumour was that a boy had intercepted a brown 'plain sealed package' addressed to the Headmaster, extracted the condoms and pricked holes in each one with a pin. Then re-sealed the package and delivered it with the Christmas cards. I have no idea whether this was true or not but the story created much laughter in the Monitor's Room when it was discerned that the Headmaster's wife was 'unexpectedly expecting'.

My last year at school was a joy because the Maths Upper VI form was a small group with Hobob Clarke as form master. It was more of a club than a class as Hobob would join in all kind of discussions as well as the formal teaching. It was not the high-pressure regime which now seems to accepted for the A-level year and we had plenty of time to play cricket. I think most of us got good results in Advanced Maths at Higher

Certificate level (later renamed as A-Level) in May 1945, which indicated that Hobob was an inspiring teacher.

Another feature which we took for granted was the venerable age of some of the teachers, brought back into service because the younger ones were in the forces. 'Pimps' Hansel was a retired chemistry teacher and rather deaf. At exam time there were always questions about the correct use of file paper and similar details. The stress of exams made bladder control more difficult :-

Boy in back row: *"Please can I go to the toilet, Sir?"*
'Pimps' :   *"Yes, use both sides of the paper."*

Huge outbreak of mirth from the whole class, leaving Mr. Hansel mystified and irritated.

Another excerpt from a letter home on 11 June 1944, the month of the Allied landings in Normandy, indicates that some major events did make an impact on me :-

' Isn't it marvellous about the invasion and I do hope they keep on advancing, once they are stopped it will mean a long drawn out affair like Italy, I expect. A boy who left the school last summer was brought back (to Bedford) a day or two ago, badly wounded. He has since died ...   What a great pity it is that we shall have to lose so many men..... We were to have gone to Haileybury on Thursday but the Head thought, quite rightly, that it would look rather bad to see a cricket team knocking about London the day after the invasion had started. With any luck we shall go this Thursday ....'

I played a lot of cricket and was wicket-keeper in the !st.XI for my last two summers, 1944 and 1945. The County Cricket league was suspended for part of the war and so we had fixtures with scratch sides including county players, probably in the Forces and stationed nearby.   On one occasion the opposition included R.W.V.Robins who had captained England against New Zealand in 1937. He bowled leg-breaks and had us schoolboys tied-up in knots. Having taken a few wickets, he said he would not bowl any more as it would finish the match too quickly. However, the captain told him to carry on bowling. An argument ensued and Robins sat down on the wicket and bluntly refused to bowl. I can't remember how it ended but it was good theatre for the crowd of local people who had come to watch these well-known players. Learie Constantine, a lovely West Indian fast bowler, also played against us on one occasion and gave friendly advice to our bowlers.

The only boy with whom I kept in touch for many years was Martin Simons. His parents had escaped from Nazi Germany with their two boys shortly before war was declared, so he was much more aware of the reality and horror of it than the rest of us on our tight little island. Martin was given a hard time at school because he spent many hours studying the daily paper to keep up with war news, instead of 'mucking about on the playing field'. In the summer of 2011, seventy years on, Martin and I paid a nostalgic visit to the School and our boarding house, now full of the sons of wealthy folk from south-east Asia, each in a separate bedsitter. No dormitories, no corporal punishment, and an altogether more civilised lifestyle. They iron their own shirts and each have at least one laptop and sometimes two, as a back-up.

"Decent hols", we used to shout to each other on the last day of the term. I returned home to Wortley in slow blacked-out trains. During those dark wartime days, when a German invasion was expected, my father was working long hours at Fox's then returning for a hasty supper before setting out on what seemed endless Home Guard exercises on the moors around

Wortley.   Initially our landlord, Lord Wharncliffe, was in charge of the local Home Guard unit, as by right as the lord of the manor, but he soon realised that military administration was not his forte and it interfered with his pheasant shooting, so he demoted himself to Lieutenant and recommended that dad be promoted to Major, a significant role for which he was well -equipped.   However, dad was obsequious in the presence of the peerage and although they were colleagues and almost friends, it led to some bizarre exchanges.   Lord Wharncliffe saluted and dad returned the salute :-

Lord W: *"Good evening, Major, where are we to go to-night?"*
Dad: *"Good evening your Lordship, we have an exercise at Crane Moor."*
Lord W: *"Ha! George Hinchcliffe, the farmer there, owes me several months rent.   I'll get it out of him."*
Dad :   *" Lieutenant Wharncliffe, I must remind you that this is a military exercise in preparation for a possible German invasion. You are under my command and there will be no opportunities for rent-collecting."*
Lord W: *"Come off it, David, don't take me too seriously."*

My father's life was so exhausting at this time , as he was very conscientious, that I thought he would not live for long after the war, but in fact he died at age 86, several years after my mother. During the war I think he had daydreams about the future for us children, 'if we can just get this Nazi regime defeated.' He wanted my brother David to develop his talent for drawing by becoming an architect, which in due course he did after a struggle with the maths exams. David reckoned his best ever work was a series of architectural drawings of Wortley Hall, a Georgian mansion, which he completed for his degree project at Liverpool University.

Lord Wharncliffe was generous towards David and me. In his amazing gun room he showed us his matched pair of Purdey shot guns and lent us smaller 20-bore guns, arranging for the head keeper, Jim Lane, to show us how to shoot pheasants.

Soon afterwards he invited us to join a day's rough shooting with some of his friends. We stood in line abreast while the keepers drove the pheasants out of the wood towards us. I blazed away without hitting any of them and, excited by the sport, turned to try again as they flew over the line. This transgressed the sacred law of shooting, never to fire 'down the line'. Lord Wharncliffe was rightly furious and shouted, " Jim, get that boy out of here before he bloody kills us all. He's more dangerous than Rommel."

Later he gave me a Game Book to record my bag, and wrote on the flyleaf :-

> *R.Sawtell from Wharncliffe   1941*
>
> *Never never let your gun*
> *Pointed be at anyone.*
> *For all the pheasants ever bred*
> *Will not repay for one man dead.*

I was forgiven and in due course he invited David and me to help to cull the herd of red deer on the estate, so we stalked and shot one each. I was haunted by the beautiful and terrified eyes of the dead stag and soon realised that I never wanted to shoot any birds or animals again, so the Game Book ends abruptly in April 1944 and the rest of it remains blank to this day.

Archie Wharncliffe was knowledgeable about animals and birds and had a strange assortment of friends who came to stay, seeming to have little to do with the war effort. There was a raffish character called Mr. Cornelius who announced in His Lordship's presence that "Archie has been searching for a double-breasted backchat".

In April 1944 Lord Wharncliffe gave me a present of six golf lessons with the professional at the local club and for some years I became an enthusiastic and competent golfer, comfortably a better player than my father or brother.
Like riding a bicycle, a good golf swing, once learned, is ingrained for life and those early lessons ensured that I could have continued to play to a reasonable standard, thanks to His Lordship's generosity. If things had turned out differently, I might easily have become a typical lifelong golfer, shouting jolly remarks across the clubroom and abandoning wife and kids to go on golfing holidays to Spain.

Dad assumed I would become a captain of industry and, at one stage, it looked as if this might happen and I would invite him to the Cutler's Feast, but by the time he died in 1973, I had 'downsized' myself and was manager of Trylon, an employee-owned outfit of a dozen people, as described hereafter. He never expressed much disappointment in me, but I think he regretted the way I had turned out. For Nancy I think he had a daydream of her sitting demurely at a grand piano in front of French windows looking out on to spacious lawns and a lake beyond. Her doting husband, possibly a minor peer or at least a wealthy barrister, was standing beside her, admiring her playing. I don't think Nancy ever accepted this idyll and, although she had piano lessons, like we all did, none of us played much subsequently. I can manage nothing more than chopsticks with the grandchildren, two of whom are Grade 8.

The BBC Symphony Orchestra was evacuated to Bedford for the duration of the war and used the Great Hall for their broadcasts. We were allowed to creep quietly into the gallery to listen and I must have heard some wonderful concerts. Sir Adrian Boult was the resident conductor and listening to him taking the rehearsals was even better than the final performance because we heard his instructions to the players. There were numerous prestigious guest soloists. A more musical boy than me would have got much more from this wonderful opportunity. When they returned to London they gave a farewell concert for the whole school and Sir Adrian invited our music teacher, Dr. Probert Jones, to conduct a trumpet fanfare he had written for the occasion.

I left Bedford in 1945, the summer in which the war ended, and went to Glasgow to sit an exam for a university scholarship in marine engineering and naval architecture, annually awarded by Denny Brothers, a small high-quality shipbuilder based on the Clyde estuary. I never knew if I had won it because, before the result was announced, news arrived that I had been awarded a State Bursary on the Higher Certificate results and this would enable me to take up a place at Clare College, Cambridge. My parents and I were all delighted at this unexpected opportunity to follow in my father's footsteps as a Cambridge engineer. The prestigious academic awards were State Scholarships and College Scholarships, and the scholars read the Latin grace before dinner in Hall every evening, whereas State Bursaries were a kind of subsidiary award for those who did not have the money to pay the full fees. The welfare state had come to my aid !

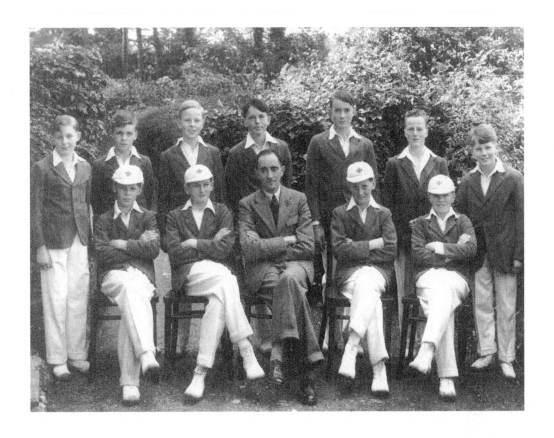

Arnold House   1st.XI   July 1940
Front row l.to r., Henry Marten, John Sandham,
Mr.Wood, Roger Sawtell, Keighley Peach

Bedford School.   Maths VI Form (Hobob Clarke) 1945

The Parsons Marine Steam Turbine Coy., Limited,

TURBINIA WORKS,
(TEL. WALLSEND 63261)
          WALLSEND-ON-TYNE.

Telegraphic Address :
" Turbinia." Wallsend.

OUR REF......JHB/JH.

YOUR REF.....................

MEMO. To

Friday, 16th May, 1947.

TO WHOM IT MAY CONCERN.

          This is to certify that ROGER DEWICK SAWTELL
received practical training in these works in the capacity of
Student Engineer from the 8th July 1946 until the 29th August 1946.
          His instruction comprised general workshop practice
including both machine and bench work.

J. H. Baxter.

Welfare Superintendent.

Parsons steam turbine, about 1900.
English Electric turbines for power stations
were still based on this design, 50 years later

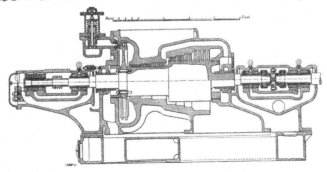

**Work experience at Parsons Marine Steam Turbine Co
Wallsend-on-Tyne   1947**

English Electric

This is to Certify

that   R. D. SAWTELL

has completed a **GRADUATE APPRENTICESHIP of**

TWO   years duration with The English Electric

Company Limited to their satisfaction

TRAINING

PATTERN SHOP, FOUNDRY, TURBINE BLADING, PROGRESS,
FACTORY EXPENSE, ERECTING SHOP, HEAVY MACHINE
SHOP, GAS TURBINE TEST, SITE ERECTION,

DoBlack   EDUCATION OFFICER   **RUGBY**   WORKS

Given under the Common Seal of the Company this

Twenty-fourth day of *October* , 19⁵⁰

*The Common Seal of The English Electric Company
Limited was affixed in the presence of*

DIRECTOR

SECRETARY

Graduate Apprenticeship at English Electric Co., Rugby.
1948-1950   Certificate signed by C.P.Snow.

Dad.   Poole Harbour 1922

FREJA at Fowey, Cornwall, with Derek Grayson. 1955
(note that Dad has bequeathed his battered hat to me)

G   CLARE COLLEGE CAMBRIDGE. 1945 – 1948 (18-21)

Before being accepted at Clare College I had to sit a College entrance exam with about fifty other candidates. The Master, Henry Thirkill, welcomed us all, handed out the exam papers and then left the room and did not reappear until two hours later, to collect the papers. The braver spirits had by then collaborated to agree on the best answers. In retrospect, we need not have bothered because I don't believe anyone even read our papers. It was a convenient ruse for Thirkill to choose by interview and then say to those not chosen that they had 'failed the Entrance Exam'.

Leaving the rather cosy situation of Bedford School and starting at university in October 1945 was a strange experience. Not only was I in a totally new educational and cultural environment but those of us straight from school were in a small minority because most of the new starters were demobbed from the armed services, anything up to five years older than us and, of course, with worldwide experiences, sometimes horrible experiences, that were quite beyond our knowledge. While we were naive and sometimes frivolous, they were serious, determined to catch up on the lost years, worked hard, and did not seem to speak much of their wartime happenings. We had little in common and so our small minority tended to stay together. It was also a time of deprivation as food and fuel were in shorter supply during the years immediately afterwards than they had been during the war itself.   The country was exhausted and, to many people's surprise, rejected the war hero Churchill and elected a Labour Government under the unprepossessing figure of Clement Attlee. Looking back now, it was a wise decision. Attlee, educated at a public school and Oxford, is regarded as one of the few ground-breaking statesmen of the 20th century and had the courage to appoint Aneurin Bevan, a fiery trade union leader, as minister of health. Bevan introduced the National Health Service, in the teeth of determined opposition from doctors.

I had a corner room in Clare Memorial Court, designed by Giles Gilbert Scott before the advent of central heating. With a miniscule coal ration it was impossible to keep warm so I augmented the open fire with a converted primus stove running on paraffin. To the familiar roar of the primus was added the pervasive smell of paraffin and the danger of knocking it over which might have set fire to the whole building. Most days, walking back from our lectures at the Department of Engineering I stopped to queue for a lardycake at Fitzbillies but the supply was inadequate so bread would often have to suffice. Dinner in Hall was strictly supervised by the Kitchen Manager, Mr Parsons, who claimed to know every student by name, and weeded out those who tried to get a 'double-dinner'.

I was introduced to squash by Ken Mayne who became a lifelong friend. It was a good way to get warm over a long cold winter and we survived. I enjoyed being an independent student; the work was interesting and I got a 1st class pass for the year but must then have been diverted by other benefits of independence and was mortified by a 3rd class pass at the end of the second year. My father told me to go back to Cambridge for a month of the long summer vacation and do some more studying without too many student diversions.

I was due to finish at Cambridge in June 1948. There was a shortage of graduate engineers in industry and during my last term a Government edict arrived proclaiming that anyone who got First Class Honours or a 2:1 would be exempted from National Service. The war had been over for three years and we all wanted to get on with our careers so we began to work long hours on revision, far into the night. The weekend before the final exams I felt mentally exhausted, so I booked myself into a small hotel near Hunstanton on the Norfolk coast and spent two days, without my books, playing golf and walking alone on the huge beaches.   It was a good decision because I finished up with a 2.1 in the Mechanichal Sciences Tripos, as good as I could expect because I was never in danger of getting a First. I was relieved with this result as the Clare engineers of my year were a valued group of friends but we were not an academically brilliant bunch.   Only one of our straight-from-school group got a First and most had to be satisfied with 2:2 or 3.   One of my friends was awarded a Special, which sounded very grand but, in fact, meant that he had failed the Honours course and was given a Pass degree. On his CV, 'Special' probably looked just as good as 'Honours', so he had no complaints.

The Cambridge academic tradition defied all logic in that this engineering degree was a BA, Bachelor of Arts, not a BSc.
On 11 June 1948 the University conferred an honorary Doctor of Letters on Winston Churchill and BA(Hons) on a few hundred others, including me. Some years later, by paying a few pounds, I was able to turn it into an MA. So I am a Master of Arts without any academic achievement beyond a first degree and without any competence in what are normally regarded as arts subjects rather than science ones.

Not everyone got through these exam hoops without trouble. My friend Pat Swash realised within minutes of the termination of the exam in machine drawing that he had inadvertently put his plan view above the elevation view. This is the American convention whereas the British practice is always to place the plan below the elevation. It was far too late to change it, so he wrote in beautiful copper-plate across the bottom of the sheet, *American Convention, a Tribute to our Great Allies*.
Memories of the vital part that US forces had played in winning the war in Europe were still very much alive in 1948 and Pat passed without question.

They were good years and I have been glad to keep in touch with Clare College since, returning for a sabbatical term in 1966 as will be related. In 1975 I organised a 30-year reunion for eight of us to compare notes and talk about old times. I noted on the programme that this same group should meet again exactly thirty years on, 11 October 2005, but this did not happen and by then two had died. The remainder have now long retired and keep in touch at Christmas but may not have the energy to get to further reunion dinners. At the last dinner I attended, one was carried out of the dining hall on a stretcher, having suffered a heart attack, and others of our year looked rather uncertain.

H ENGLISH ELECTRIC Co.Ltd. 1948-1950 (21-23)

Together with several friends, I decided to sign-up for a two year graduate apprenticeship at the Rugby works of English Electric Ltd., part of a large industrial combine.   Apart from holiday work, harvesting and fruit picking, this was my first paid work. *

* My last paid work was at Daily Bread Co-operative where I finally
  retired in 1997,aged 70, a total of 48 years which earned me a
  maximum standard State Pension, but no occupational pension,
  due to the peculiar nature of my so-called career.

The chairman of English Electric was Sir George Nelson. His son, colloquially known as 'half-nelson', was managing director, an example of nepotism which was strange in what was a large and influential business.   They were both based at the Stafford works where electric motors and heavy-duty alternators were manufactured . The director in charge of the Rugby works was Michael Price who had married the Chairman's daughter.   The senior managers, from Stafford and Rugby would often hold meetings on the morning train to London and, on arrival at Euston, Sir George went about his business and the rest went straight back to Stafford or Rugby on the next train to get on with the day's work.

Graduate Apprentices were paid six guineas (£6.6.0) per week and my lodgings cost two pounds, for which my landlady provided breakfast and supper, all meals at weekends, and all my washing including the oil-stained 'boiler suits' we wore at work. She had three clever daughters who were all away doing degrees and Ph.D's but sometimes came home at weekends. I suspected that she thought I might 'take up' with one of them, but I resisted any such temptation because it might interfere with cricket in the summer or squash in the winter. I bought a made-to-measure dinner jacket and added the trousers a few months later when a few more pounds had accumulated in my bank account. It was a good investment as I was still able to wear it at a college reunion dinner sixty years later. I even took out a life insurance policy and paid £27 per year into it for many years, after which it yielded a substantial sum, far in excess of my contributions.

At the Rugby works English Electric made four types of prime mover, steam turbines, water turbines, large diesel engines, and gas turbines. Such comprehensive training opportunities under one roof were unlikely to be offered anywhere else in the world and the regime was not especially demanding. We were each attached to a skilled tradesman, usually a fitter or machinist and sometimes given responsible work. I nearly ruined a large diameter cast steel blade ring for a steam turbine destined for Abadan, in what is now Iran, by machining too much off the diameter. The inspector was surprisingly accommodating about it and rather than blasting-off about allowing 'college lads' to operate large machine tools, he had it welded-up and I got it right on the second attempt.

The men at Rugby Works were generally friendly but there were some exceptions. The storekeeper was notorious for being bad tempered. On one occasion I was sent to the stores to get a particular bolt, urgently required to finish a component:-

"Sorry, it's not available," said the storekeeper.
"But I can see it on the shelf behind you," I said.
"Yes, you can, smartarse, but it's not available, see.
   Mr Price has told me to always have one in stock and if I give

it to you I won't have it in stock, will I ?"
" But ....'
*" Don't give me any buts, young fella. You may have letters
after your name but I know my job here, so just keep bloody
quiet in the presence of your elders and betters."*

I was very impressed with the skill of some of the men to
whom I was attached. Pattern makers could turn a complex
drawing into a series of wooden patterns, often with several
cores, from which the moulds for castings were made. The
pattern maker had to think in three dimensions and he had also
to be a skilled woodworker to make the patterns to accurate
dimensions. An artist turns three dimensions into two on canvas
but a pattern maker turns two dimensions into three, in wood.
My job, as an apprentice, was to rough out some of the
woodwork ready for the pattern maker to finish it to limits
totally beyond my ability. They would swear at the drawing
office people for making mistakes and whistle nonchalantly as
they went about their manual work. These highly intelligent
men had had no option but to leave school at fifteen while I
had had the privilege of free education until twenty one. I was
overawed by their competence and embarrassed at this
educational injustice because I considered that several of
them would have been capable of getting first class degrees.
In due course their sons and daughters would have this
opportunity. When my time in the pattern shop was ended, I
invited the two I had been working with for a thank-you drink
at their local pub. They were keen trade unionists and when we
were thrown out at closing time, I knew a good deal about the
Union of Pattern Makers and pondered on the issues of fair
pay and equal opportunities. A seminal experience for me.
Later, as I shall relate, when I was a front-line department
manager at Spear & Jackson in Sheffield, I was again involved
with skilled tradesmen, particularly saw-makers, discussing

their work, negotiating rates of pay, chairing disciplinary procedures, playing cricket for the works team. I respected their knowledge and intelligence and realised how little, as a business, we valued them.

Back at Rugby, when my mentor had no particular need for my, often clumsy, assistance, I was able to wander round the works absorbing all manner of machines and processes and social encounters. He would say, "*Always carry a spanner, lad, then the bosses will assume you are working.*"

I spent some months in the steam turbine department where English Electric were building their first 60 MW generating set, with a hydrogen-cooled alternator made at the Stafford works. It had three turbines, high pressure, intermediate and low pressure. They were manufactured and assembled in the fitting shop at Rugby then dismantled and rebuilt on site, in this case at Stourport on Severn, near Birmingham. I recollect being very impressed by these massive machines and the close tolerances required in their manufacture. It was mechanical engineering at its best and I jumped at the chance of spending the last month of my apprenticeship, May 1950, on site, assembling and testing Stourport B. We got the set going and I was allocated to the night shift during a week when the boiler suppliers, Babcock & Wilcox, were testing their equally huge equipment.

One night the English Electric foreman in charge of us apprentices fell sick and I found myself the senior person, looking after this enormous machine, with two other apprentices. Usually this would be routine with no problems expected but, in the middle of the night, the boiler people had a technical fault and told us that, in a few minutes, there would be no steam. This meant that we had to shut down the turbines and although we had a comprehensive operating manual on the procedures to be followed, there was no time to phone the English Electric site manager, Peter, at the hotel where he was staying. So, with the manual in one hand and a spanner in the other, we tried to follow the procedure for Emergency Shutdown. I knew that the critical factor was the steam glands on the high pressure rotor. These are fins on the rotor shaft which fit into grooves in the casing, to minimise the escape of steam. The clearance between the rotating fin and the static casing is very small and varies with the temperature of the rotor. As part of the running-in routine we had to read this clearance through a telescope fixed to the casing and record it every hour in thousandths of an inch. The problem with an emergency shutdown was that, without steam, the rotor cools rapidly and the discs may come in contact with the casing, in which case there would be serious damage and the rotor, weighing several tonnes, would have to be dismantled and returned to Rugby for repair. This would entail weeks of delay and considerable expense, so I was glued to this telescope, watching the clearance and shouting to the others who were manning the steam valves, using what steam we had to slow the rotor as gradually as possible.   It took about an hour for the rotor to run down from its working speed of 3000 rpm to stationary and we managed to control it sufficiently to avoid damage. Peter, an experienced turbine engineer, arrived in his pyjamas to find the three of us quivering wrecks with the anxiety but pleased that we had managed the emergency without damaging the turbine.

A few days later, Michael Price, the main board Director in charge of the Rugby turbine works, visited Stourport and congratulated us but said we should never have been left in charge without an experienced engineer. He then offered me a job. English Electric was a large company with many layers of management and had recently appointed the novelist, C P Snow, to be Personnel Director. Snow was an urbane figure and when I told him I had in mind to accept an alternative job offer from a smaller company he said, "*I assume you want to be a bigger fish in a smaller pond.*" I think he was right and although several of my friends stayed with English Electric, some for the whole of their working lives, I have never regretted my decision to move to Spear & Jackson in Sheffield in 1950. At that time, I was a well-qualified ambitious young man and wanted to climb the management ladder as quickly as possible.

I   SPEAR & JACKSON Ltd.   1950-1966   (23-39)

The grimy works of Spear & Jackson, tool and steel makers since 1760, was located in the Don Valley, east of the centre of Sheffield, world-renowned for special steel-making.

The historical view was that the Don Valley was the best place for industry as the prevailing wind was from the west so that the smoke was blown to Rotherham, which we Sheffield folk regarded as no more or less than they deserved. The Victorian catalogues had engravings showing numerous chimneys belching black smoke. This was a deliberate sales pitch meaning, '*We are busy with orders. Get yours in quickly or you will go to the back of the queue*'.

In 1950, both the managing director and the sales director were descendants of the original Jackson dynasty and both seemed to have an in-born aptitude for steel technology and the market which had kept the company prosperous for generations. They relied on Yorkshire common sense and were slightly suspicious of 'book learning'. On the shop floor, 'Spears' was regarded as a good place to work because redundancy was very rare and the products were shipped all over the world so that when one market was diminishing, another was expanding. Good quality steel tools for agriculture and woodworking were always in demand. However, technology was becoming more than common sense could bear and so they hired me as the first graduate engineer to be employed by the business in nearly 200 years.

I had some superficial knowledge of steelworks bosses because, as children, we had often been to Sheffield to visit Jack and Isa Grant, friends of my parents. They lived at Dore

Moor House, west of the city centre away from the smoke, and I thought their house and lifestyle was the best thing I had ever seen. Each room had paired doors so that one could hide in the dark space between them, and the huge drawing room looked out over spacious lawns and a small lake on which there was a boat which we were allowed to row backwards and forwards 'across the sea'.   Perfect for small boys. Aunt Isa was my godmother, a rather formidable chain-smoking person but she was hospitable and kind to me. Jack (later Sir John) Grant was a genial steel baron and special to me because he had his own squash court in the stable block at Dore, and continued to play until all his daughters could beat him. After that he soon died.   All this, the large house, the spacious garden, lake, squash court, convinced me, aged ten, that this was the perfect life and I resolved to be a steelworks boss when I grew up. Now in 1950, aged 23, I had the opportunity in front of me and assumed I would stay in Sheffield for the rest of my working life.

On moving from Rugby to Sheffield I returned to live at home with my parents at Wortley and travelled the ten miles to work on a BSA 250cc motor bike which Spear & Jackson had bought during the war for the director's use, as petrol was very short and rationed. However, in the winter I got the tyres stuck in tram lines more than once, and after a few early morning spills I abandoned the bike. Soon afterwards my father retired and my parents moved to Hampshire, so our long attachment to Wortley ended and I moved into lodgings in Sheffield. For a time my digs were in Dore village, not far from the fabled Dore Moor House but by this time it was no longer privately owned and had become a guest house for one of the large steel companies. Inevitably it was more of an institution with notices everywhere and no boat on the lake. Perhaps my dream house and the culture which went with it were already fading, even though I had only recently started to climb the management ladder at Spear & Jackson.

When I arrived, in September 1950, I was put to work with Walter Helliwell, Chief Draughtsman. He came from a humble background, had never worked anywhere else and had progressed by innate intelligence and hard work, of which he was rightly proud. Walter had an extensive vocabulary of Yorkshire swearwords, some of which are too strong for these pages. He had been in a reserved occupation during the war, as Spear & Jackson were making tools for the war effort, but in 1945, as part of the surrender reparations, he was kitted out in a colonel's uniform and sent to the Ruhr Valley to see what we could learn from German industry. He liked to relate how he had been a 'proper colonel without knowing one end of a rifle from the other' and said, "*You can call me Colonel Helliwell if you like but most people here just refer to me as that bloody Walter."*

One day the Chairman was chivvying him to complete a special machine and Walter picked up the phone to a supplier and yelled: "*What the bloody hell is stopping you delivering those ******* bearings we are waiting for ?"*
"*What is Mr Helliwell shouting about?"* asked the Chairman.
"*He's speaking to a supplier in Birmingham, sir",* said I.
"*Well, tell him to use the telephone",* said the Chairman.

Walter was a brilliant designer and some of his special machines for sawmaking were ingenious. The Germans had little to teach him. He designed machinery for grinding the first inserted-tooth circular saws for our subsidiary company in Vancouver, serving the lumber industry on the west coast of Canada and USA, and he revolutionised the machine setting of handsaw teeth which had traditionally been a highly specialised manual skill with a setting hammer. Had he had the opportunity he would have got a first class degree in engineering design and though, outwardly, he disparaged my academic training, I think he secretly acknowledged the value of it. As a 'raw college lad' I was never a threat to Walter . We became good friends and when I was Works Director, I was glad to promote him to be Chief Engineer.

In the 1950's, with worldwide orders flowing into the sales office, increasing production was the priority and my task was to mechanise some of the time-honoured manual skills of sawmaking. The process of which I am still proud was the production of bowsaw blades. It started with steel strip in a coil and the first operation was to cut it into short lengths so that each blade could be set and sharpened on a series of machines, each operated by one man. My design, in co-operation with Walter, was to process the whole coil by passing it continuously from one machine to the next in an oval layout, controlled by one man in the middle. The last operation was to cut it into the required lengths. This 'saved' at least six men who could be transferred to other work. Our publicity department hailed it as 'automation' and showed it off to numerous visitors as an example of a traditional manufacturer hauling itself into the 20th century. I still have the sketches of the feeding mechanism, and several patents that we took out to prevent our competitors catching up with us,

I discovered I was more interested in people than design , asked to be transferred to production and was appointed assistant manager of the handsaw department. Spear & Jackson had an enviable reputation for top quality handsaws and we exported them all over the world. Our only serious competitors were Disston in Philadelphia USA and Sandvik in Sweden. The Directors were not sure what to do with me so they sent me to visit our subsidiaries in Vancouver and Eugene, near Portland. While in USA I decided to visit Disston to see what I could learn.   I was shown into the office of the Executive Vice President and, with the naivity of a 24 year old, asked him to show me round the works, knowing that they had developed some state-of-the-art sawmaking manufacturing processes.   He appeared nonplussed at such cheek from a competitor but recovered his composure and said *'Sure'.* We then got into his car and he drove me slowly round the perimeter track of their large works and then took me out to lunch and back to the station. *"I'm happy to have taken you round our facility, Mr Sawtell. Goodbye."* I never got inside the works at all. A learning experience.

Back in the handsaw department I got on well with Jack Adsetts, the Manager who had at least 40 years service behind him. In the office he smoked a pipe, as many did at that time, despite the fact that there was a considerable fire risk because saw handles were made from kiln-dried beech blocks. (Years later we installed an injection moulding machine and changed over to plastic, apart from the top of the range which were still made from rosewood.) The foreman in charge of this section was Alf Westwood who knew more about saw handles than anyone else in UK and supervised a group of men who cut out the handles on router machines, and about twenty young women who did the finishing operations. Alf made sure that each work station was sufficiently far from the adjacent one so that the operators could not talk to each other above the high-pitched whirr of the sanding machines. Alf was also a surrepticious smoker and one night fire broke out and the whole workshop was burned out.

I was then given the task of getting a new building put up urgently and recommending a new production line.   My plan was that we should put the finishing machines in clusters of four instead of a linear conveyor belt. "*Nay Mester Roger*," said Alf, "*that'll never do. Them wenches will do nowt but chitter to each other. I know 'em. We'll not get the same work out of 'em.*" However, the Works Director over-ruled him, saying "*Let the lad have his head, Alf. He's got to learn.*" So I spent much time planning this new production line, determined to make it work. The 'wenches' liked the idea of clusters and they certainly did chitter but within weeks the productivity figures exceeded the previous layout and went on increasing for months. When Jack retired, I was promoted to Department Manager and thereafter to Works Manager. In due course I was invited to join the Board as Works Director. I was 29. Alf was apprehensive and said "*He's a young 'un with an old 'un's head on 'is shoulders.*"

The works entrance was a brick arch with double gates protected by a massive iron bollard on each side, scored with the marks of horse-drawn drays which had cut the corner too fine a hundred years ago and paid the penalty. Alongside was a small door marked 'Visitors'. It had a brass plaque which had originally displayed 'SPEAR & JACKSON' but daily cleaning and polishing for a century had all but obliterated the letters and, in my time, it looked like ' EAR & JACK '. This door led to a narrow staircase at the top of which sat Mrs Smith, the much-feared telephone operator. She was protected by a sliding window which she kept tight shut if she disapproved of a visitor. There was no other way of communicating with her.
We never had anyone remotely called a receptionist, Mrs Smith reigned supreme, and sometimes there would be several disconsolate sales representatives sitting on the horsehair bench, waiting for her to condescend to open the window.

The switchboard consisted of an array of plugs attached to spring-loaded cables.   Mrs Smith inserted the plugs into appropriate sockets for each call connected. I can still hear the *zip* as the plugs sprang back into their parking places when she disconnected a call. At the height of her powers, which coincided with a time of frantic postwar production, she was like an organist, connecting and disconnecting countless outgoing calls per minute. She answered incoming enquiries with equal rapidity and sometimes the caller only heard ' ear and jackson', similar to the plaque on the street door. This was the east end of Sheffield and we called her the fastest gun in the east.

Mrs Smith took a motherly interest in me when I arrived as a young graduate, and we remained friendly colleagues as I rose within the company establishment. Her support was important as she would put my calls through without delay whereas those to whom she took a dislike had difficulty in making any calls at all as there was no straight through dialling at that time. It was suspected that she listened in to phone conversations which interested her, not so much for picking up scandal but more to be involved in company policy and practice. 'Spears' was such an important part of her life and she was rightly proud to be the vital daily link to the world outside Savile Street. Sadly as she grew older, like many of us, she began to make mistakes and we had to ask her to retire, but she remained an oft-quoted integral part of this close-knit self-confident Yorkshire manufacturer.

In the 1950's, Germany had not yet recovered from the war, Japan was not yet a major producer and China was unheard of, so we had floods of orders from all over the world and the machine shops were working day and night. From time to time I used to go and walk round the works on the night shift; the atmosphere was more relaxed than during the day, partly because there was less supervision. One night I found Joe, a skilled machine tool operator, asleep by his machine.

"I'm tired out by trying to get the piecework done", he said. Summoning all the pretentious gravitas I could muster, I said, *"Your job is to maximise production, tired or not. You are suspended until further notice. Go home."*

A year later, during the day shift, as I was passing his machine at tea break, he called me over and handed me a tin cup, *"It's our anniversary,"* he said, *"it's just a year since you suspended me for being asleep on the job. No hard feelings. Have a cup of tea. And by the way I think these circular saws I'm working on for Vancouver could be improved if we used a softer grade of grinding wheel. What do you think?"*

Many of the machine operators had been with the company for years and took pride in the products but it was not the culture at that time for Directors to be on such easy terms with shop floor workers. We made the decisions and it would not have occurred to my boardroom colleagues to seek the views of a machine operator. However, this small incident was one of many which brought me to realise how much the success of the business depended on skilled men who had had no further education beyond fifteen. Their grandchildren would go to universities but they had had no such option. Spear & Jackson offered stable employment and a clock to go on the mantelpiece after fifty years service. But managers and manual workers also antagonised one another by the rivalries and duplicity of piecework and this form of payment humiliated and diminished many well-intentioned men and women.

Jimmy Reid, a well-known Marxist shop steward at a Clydebank shipyard around that time, had a nice story. He suggested a labour-saving improvement to the management who accepted it with alacrity and rewarded him with a small payment. A month later he was made redundant. When he asked why, he was told that the revised procedure enabled the job to be done with one less person.

A Director of Firth Brown, a large steel firm next door to us, told me that one of their most outspoken shop stewards turned up at the company AGM. The Chairman was horrified and asked how he came to be there.

" *I used my bonus to buy a few shares. I got three for five pounds* ", he said.

" *Well,*" said the Chairman, "*I'll give you ten pounds for them.*" A year later, Smithers was there again at the AGM, asking some awkward questions.

" *Well, it's like this, Mr Crosby, I used your ten pounds to buy some more shares. If I go on like this, I may own the company one day.*"

I thought there must be a better way to organise work and started reading about the co-operative movement, initiated by a small group of working men in Rochdale in 1844, as an alternative structure to counteract the greed of those with capital and the degradation of manual workers in the early years of the industrial revolution.

As well as tools, we were also makers of special steels and the specifications were a closely guarded secret. At a certain point in the process the manager of the melting shop, and no one else, would produce a small envelope from an inner pocket and drop it dramatically into the white hot molten metal. Not even the managing director was privy to the nature of this secret ingredient, and nor was I, but we both suspected that it was nothing more than straightforward iron filings which had no affect on the properties of the steel but confounded any spy wanting to copy the specification. It also consolidated the job security of the melting shop manager. Looking back from fifty years on, it is extraordinary that such arcane practices were regarded as normal and legitimate in what was otherwise a highly controlled technical process.

The elite employer's organisation for Sheffield industry is The Cutler's Company, an age-old livery company no longer associated with cutlery. However, the rules and the tradition remained that every member must be associated with cutting edges. The big steel companies circumnavigated this by claiming that their maintenance departments used cutting tools, but for Spear & Jackson this rule was no problem as we were manufacturers of saws and machine knives and had been for two hundred years. The Master Cutler was elected annually and was regarded as the spokesman and leader of the Sheffield steel industry. He made a powerful trio with the Lord Mayor and the Leader of the City Council. The annual Cutler's Feast was a large ceremonial dinner with a national speaker and it was the tradition that, on the day following, the Master Cutler invited all the Members to visit the works with which he was associated.

In 1960 my boss, Stephen de Bartolomé, from whom I learned a great deal about business management, was Master Cutler and it was my job as Works Director to get the works cleaned-up and to plan the route for several hundred visitors. For the big bulk steelmakers this kind of formal visit was no problem but, as a specialised medium-sized company, we had processes which we certainly did not want our local competitors to see, so the visit had to be planned to avoid some departments such as the sawmaking machines which I had developed with Walter Helliwell and which had led to considerable gains in productivity. It was cat and mouse because, having gained entry as members of the Cutler's Company, our sharp-eyed competitors were determined to make best use of the visit.

In order to emulate Jack Grant, I had been happy to accept the invitation to become a Freeman of The Cutler's Company and therefore join the queue to be Master Cutler in due course, but during the 1960's, influenced by the Iona Community and the Sheffield Industrial Mission (SIM), my views changed. The SIM was a sustained and deeply thought out attempt by the churches, led by Bishop Leslie Hunter, to engage with people at their places of work in the steel industry. As managers we were to tease out what were called the 'middle axioms' such as fair pay, equality of opportunity, and we were to confront injustice in the workplace.

My day to day work brought me into close contact with skilled manual workers in the sawmaking departments. They were the backbone of the business and their skills, handed down from one generation to another, had enabled the company to survive through numerous slumps and recessions.   I have always enjoyed using hand tools but never achieved the kind of quality standards that sawmakers needed to maintain the Spear & Jackson reputation.

The directors took the policy decisions, of course, which were vital for the continuity of the business, but when I was appointed to the Board only two of us spent much time on the shop floor, the director of the steel melting department and myself.   I was daily involved with the practicalities of producing tools for a worldwide market, planning production runs, setting hourly rates and piecework prices, dealing with discipline procedures, settling 'border disputes'.   I was endlessly impressed with the intelligence and common sense of these men.   It was often my task to make the presentation of a clock for long service and I realised the absence of opportunities to fulfil their potential. I noted that their sons, but not yet their daughters, were just beginning to go to universities instead of straight into manual work.

For example, I got to know George Bradshaw, our finest saw sharpener and setter. With a hammer he had made himself, with a very narrow face, he could set a tenon saw with 20 teeth to the inch in less than a minute and the result was better than the machine setting of cheap saws. This was not a secret process and I often asked George to demonstrate his skill to visitors which he was glad to do, as a respite from piecework. But George had also thought out how to improve the setting machines by modifying the anvils to give a 'kinder' and therefore stronger set. I sought his advice when working on the idea of joining up the setting and sharpening machines into a continuous process. This had led to a huge increase in productivity and I got the credit for it, but I knew that it was based on George's experience as much as mine. In due course, I presented him with his long service clock and he was proud to receive it, but the injustice troubled my conscience. To the surprise of some friends, I became very interested in developing shared decision-making in the workplace and equality of opportunities.

By 1964, aged 37, I was Deputy Managing Director and virtually in charge of the main works in Savile Street, Sheffield, as Stephen Bartolomé was involved in buying-up other toolmaking companies in UK and expanding our presence in Canada, USA, India and South Africa, to convert Spear & Jackson from a local business into an international company, small by stock market standards but prestigious and profitable for the benefit of the shareholders, mostly a handful of retired directors or their widows who seldom, if ever, darkened the doors of our grimy premises in the Don Valley.

When the Chairman retired in 1966, Stephen Bartolomé moved up to be Chairman and the Board offered me the job of Managing Director, at which, as an ambitious young man, I had been aiming for the best part of sixteen years. This was a considerable break with tradition because there had never been a managing director from outside the Jackson family and I was aware of the confidence my colleagues were investing in me. I said yes, but on the understanding that I would have the support of the Board in turning the company into a much more participative business , with high levels of shared decision-making with the shop floor, employee-shareholding and other radical changes. My Board colleagues were not surprised because they had watched me moving in this direction for some time, but when it came to the crunch, they said 'no', this was altogether too risky for a business with our reputation, and by the way, the outside shareholders would not like it. I was upset and angry for I knew that this was a wonderful opportunity for a radical change and that I had gained the experience to make a go of it. However, I realised that I had little chance of winning the boardroom debate and making significant changes, even with some backing from my friend and mentor, Stephen, who now had wider responsibilities as Chairman of what had become a group of companies with works in six different countries worldwide.

So I gave in my notice, in a huff, without having any plan of what to do next. Stephen was understandably irritated at my refusal because he knew my ambitions and had every reason to suppose I would jump at the opportunity. They gave me a clock as a leaving present and searching for something neutral to say at the presentation ceremony he claimed I was probably the last person to know almost everyone at the Sheffield works by name. The company was expanding so he was probably right. A new managing director was subsequently appointed from Scotland and instituted a very different regime. He did not last long.

I turned down an invitation to be chief executive of Sanderson Brothers & Newbould, one of our strongest local competitors, because they also were very apprehensive about my ideas on 'participation'. Within a week or so I received a letter from the local Labour Exchange notifying me that I was eligible for unemployment benefit. Although not short of money, because I had been well paid at Spear & Jackson, I went to collect this benefit for a few weeks, as an experience. It was a time of prosperity in Sheffield and jobs were available, but the men in the queue seemed anxious and despondent. I realised the importance of having work, for self-confidence as well as to keep food on the table. These men, including myself, wanted to feel they were capable of earning money to maintain their families. For life to have meaning, we need a purpose and I realised, for the first time, that long-term unemployment can lead not only to despondency but to despair. Much later on I had this in mind when considering security of employment for new businesses such as Trylon and Daily Bread Co-operative and we developed ways to handle recession in a quite different manner to the remote hire and fire procedures of conventional companies owned by distant equity shareholders. For example, at Daily Bread, the manager appointed by working members, is given considerable autonomy to take trading decisions quickly, but decisions regarding the conditions of employment must be referred to the weekly meeting of members.

Spear & Jackson continued for a time as an independent company but, in due course, was bought out by another prestigious Sheffield company, James Neill. Later, most of the tool production was moved overseas and it fell into the hands of anonymous asset-stripping bankers and was the subject of a major share scandal. The name remains but there is no workforce to speak of in Sheffield and the New Buildings which we proudly constructed in the 1950's have been pulled down to make room for roadworks. A sad decline but similar to numerous well-known Sheffield companies, as Japan and then China emerged as manufacturers to the world.

Spear & Jackson, with its proud tradition of quality tools for over 250 years, were bought by a Chinese company in 2014.

The CORBY BUILDING at Spear & Jackson Ltd.,Savile Street,Sheffield.1962 Thirty years later, the whole of this huge building (Corby I and Corby II) was demolished to make room for road improvements.

Our wedding at Little Aston, Birmingham. September 1957

THE CALL TO MISSION ANSWERED

Ted Wickham and the Sheffield Industrial Mission
1944-1959

by PHILIP BLOY

Edited by Roger Sawtell

Ted Wickham (centre)   Leslie Hunter (right)

Published by   Disciples Press
                 C/o Daily Bread Co-operative Ltd.,
                 Bedford Road, Northampton NN4 7AD

                 ISBN O 946 46510 9

                 First published: October 2000
                 Second edition: April 2001

Front cover showing Ted Wickham and Leslie Hunter (Bishop of Sheffield) at a shopfloor discussion group, circa 1955.

Family at a friend's wedding.Rebecca,Peter,Mary.1971

Trylon Ltd. Wollaston, Northants. 1977 (RS 1968-74)
An employee-owned co-operative business.

J LOVE AND MARRIAGE - 1957 onwards

The matrons of Sheffield with daughters to be married, kept a close eye on the announcements of new Members of The Cutlers Company and so, as an eligible bachelor, I found myself invited to dances. Although increasingly confident in my work situation, I felt clumsy and out of place at these rather formal social occasions and the girls must have considered me priggish and supercilious. I was happier playing squash or sailing with a few close friends. Derek Grayson and I had an arrangement with the owner of a beautiful 25' sloop based near Falmouth. We carried out some of the maintenance and in return we had the use of *Freja* for our precious holidays, one week at Whitsun and two weeks in the summer if we were lucky. We sailed around the south coast and further afield to Brittany and the Channel Islands.   However, romance was on the horizon.

In 1955, my brother David, my sister Nancy and I spent our summer holiday sailing on the west coast of Scotland.   We chartered a 5-ton yacht from Oban and cruised among the wonderful Hebridean islands. One night we anchored off Iona and rowed ashore to explore, having heard there was some kind of Christian community on the island. On the quay we were advised to visit a house near the Abbey church. The door was answered by a commanding figure who, before we could say a word, exclaimed, *"Ha, I know you have come to tell me about the Apostolic Succession. You are quite wrong, of course..."* He continued to harangue us and took no notice of our protestations that we knew next to nothing about the Apostolic Succession or any other succession, we were just enquirers passing-by. Only then did we realise that we were talking to George Macleod, the Founder and Leader of the Iona

Community. It was a life-changing event for us. Here were young ministers of the Church of Scotland dedicated to working in industrial areas and concerned with issues of justice and peace. We joined as Associate Members and remained so for many years, David more involved than me. As a trainee architect he was particularly interested in the restoration of the Abbey buildings which was the initial task of the Community, and he returned later that summer as a volunteer guide to the Abbey, for the day tourists who came in their hundreds by steamer from Oban. *

* Years later, in April 2009, we scattered David's ashes on the Sound of
  Iona, just a few rope lengths from the spot where we had anchored 50
  years previously.

David phoned to say he had 'met my future wife' camping on Iona and she was working in Sheffield as an Occupational Therapist. I made haste to contact Susan and her friends, and abandoning other weekend pursuits such as cricket, we went walking in the Peak District and the following year, Derek and I invited Susan and another friend, Mary, to come sailing with us in *Freja.* On our way back from visiting the Scilly Isles we ran into very bad weather in the English Channel and only just survived , all four of us being seasick and *Freja* hove-to in a busy shipping lane. We were glad to get back to Falmouth, our home port, and learned that several yachts had been dismasted in this gale and one crew member was drowned after his boat capsized.

This test having been accomplished satisfactorily, I proposed to Susan, sheltering from the rain, under a gorse bush somewhere on the moors near Sheffield, and, joyfully, she said yes. It was me, a self-satisfied young man, who then had some hesitations which plagued me for a time. Susan, wiser than me and also influenced by Iona, had no desire to be a Sheffield society wife but I had not quite abandoned my plan to be a wealthy industrialist like Jack Grant.

Thankfully, I gradually put these boyhood ambitions behind me, and we were married by Ted Wickham in 1957.   In his homily he said he was not going to talk about *"conventional lovey-dovey wedding truisms"* but declared that Susan and I must be '*catalysts* ', a term well understood in the steel industry, causing change without getting destroyed or consumed in the process. *

* Half a century later, Susan and I were invited by the Religious Society of Friends (Quakers) to give the annual Swarthmore Lecture in 2006 and chose the title *Reflections from a Long Marriage,* subsequently published by Quaker Books (2006). Ted's words ring in our ears as we try to be catalysts and wrestle with the teachings of Jesus.

In 1957 we bought a 5-bedroom Victorian house in Sheffield for less than my annual salary at Spear & Jackson, larger and draughtier than any of our subsequent homes. Mrs Finlay, who had worked as a file grinder at Cammells when my dad was a manager there, came to help with the housework. The windows accumulated the grime from the Don Valley and Mrs Finlay cleaned them every week. She went to London for the first time, on a day trip, and reported to Susan that she had had a close look at Buckingham Palace and reckoned that 'the curtains needed a good wash'.   Fortunately she was not attracted to help the Queen with her housework and stayed with us for all the time we were in Sheffield.

When Susan and I married we took it for granted that we would have children and were delighted when they made their appearances. I do not recall any planning discussion about when might be an appropriate time. We just waited to see what would happen and ended up with four.

From friends with families we knew what to expect; endless nappies, years of parent's evenings at school, moody teenagers. We took all this in our stride, Susan more than me. What we were not prepared for was two near-death experiences and the fear generated by these has stayed with me for half a century and is unlikely to go away.

Ruth, the eldest, went to a primary school ten minutes walk from our house, on the other side of a main road. When Mary, the next one, was about three, Susan would walk to school with both of them and also Rebecca, the baby, in a pushchair. One day in 1963 as they traversed the pedestrian crossing, an oncoming double-decker bus failed to stop and the front wheel caught Mary a glancing blow on her thigh. Another few inches and she would have been killed. She was rushed to hospital. The wound healed and, although she will bear the scar all her life, she was not disfigured. We were very thankful.

The police prosecuted the bus driver and Susan was called as a witness. Roy Hattersley and I had recently been appointed as Magistrates and some of the Sheffield establishment were claiming that we were both 'far too young'. Roy was 30 and I was 35. He went on to be a Cabinet Minister at 33 and subsequently Deputy Prime Minister. I went to the court hearing as part of training for the Bench. The bus driver was convicted of dangerous driving and was fined and his licence endorsed. I learned later that the magistrates had neglected to check his record, which they should have done before sentencing, and it transpired that he had a previous conviction for careless driving. If this had been taken into account at the hearing, he would probably been disqualified from driving and would have lost his job. In retrospect, knowing how easy it is momentarily to lose concentration when driving, I was glad he was not penalised more severely. Mary was awarded £500 compensation; quite a large sum in those days.

A few years later when Peter, our youngest, was two we went on holiday to Majorca. Picnicking beside the hotel pool, I heard a shout behind me and saw that he had fallen in and was lying face upwards on the bottom of the pool. Before I could jump in, the man who had shouted had already gone to his rescue and and promptly pulled him out. I guess that Peter had not been in the water for more than a minute. We drained him off and, amazingly, he was unharmed and did not even need artificial respiration, but I shall always carry in my mind the momentary picture of him lying under water, gazing calmly upward. A frightening incident.

Our lives are very fragile. Our children survived but these experiences were unforgettable examples of vunerability. We know, from relatives and friends, that the death of a child, either from illness or from an accident, is something from which parents never completely recover.

K JOURNEY TO JERUSALEM - 1967

In 1966 when I left Spear & Jackson, we decided to use the opportunity between jobs to go travelling, but first I became a student for the Michaelmas Term at Clare College. I had not been expecting to leave Spear & Jackson so precipitously and had no idea what to do next. I had been well-paid and did not need to find work straight away so it seemed sensible to have a sabbatical time to search for the way ahead.

I wrote to Charlie Moule who had been Dean of Clare College in my undergraduate days in the 1940s and was now Lady Margaret's Professor of Divinity. He replied saying he was shortly going to USA for a sabbatical term and inviting me to live in his rooms in Clare Old Court for the Michaelmas Term, together with the services of his 'gyp' who did the housework and cleaned my shoes. Whatever he thought, he was much too discreet to indicate that he normally worked for a distinguished academic* rather than an unlettered industrial person.

*The Rev. Professor Charles Moule CBE DD FBA. The following year, on the way back from our family journey to Jerusalem, we parked our caravan behind Clare Memorial Court and Charlie, world-renowned New Testament scholar, read a bedtime story about Pooh Bear and the heffalump, to our children in their bunks. Later, he retired to Pevensey on the south coast where I visited him several times. A wonderful, inspirational, humble Christian.

I went to some lectures at the Department of Divinity with young men half my age, did some in-depth reading about the Kingdom of God, what did it mean and how did it impact work in industry. (I write more about this later, in the section Faith Journey). I was invited to dine with the Fellows and drink port with them afterwards in the Senior Common Room. A very contrasting regime to industrial Sheffield.   Across the corridor was Maurice Wiles, an authority on the Early Fathers of the Christian church, subsequently appointed Regius Professor of Divinity at Oxford in 1970.   Maurice undertook the somewhat thankless task of supervising my studies and reading my essays to assist my search. My contribution was to run him round the squash court to help keep him fit.   His son, Andrew, was a gawky schoolboy at the time and is now Sir Andrew Wiles, a brilliant mathematician who solved Fermat's Last Theorem.*   I am so grateful to both these notable scholars, Moule and Wiles for taking the trouble to spend time with me.   The term helped to clear my head about what to do for work henceforward.

* The equation , x to the power of n, plus y to the power of n, = equals z to the power of n, has no integral solutions for values of n greater than two. This problem had defeated mathematicians for two centuries.

After commuting every week or two to Cambridge, I returned home at Christmas and in February 1967 we set off to travel overland to Jerusalem with the children, in a motor caravan, a Commer Highwayman bought for the purpose. Our plan was to see some of the world by travelling slowly across Europe and the Middle East but also to visit the places where our Christian faith was founded and developed, and to experience a democratic community by living on a kibbutz for a few weeks. We asked a young woman, Carole, to come with us to help with the children and teach them whenever possible, so we were a party of seven.

My godmother, Aunt Isa, wrote me a sharply critical letter:-
  'I beg leave to doubt, as a family man, with a
  wife and four fairly small children, whether
  you are right to throw up a good job and travel .... '

I had no such doubts at the time and have no regrets now, regarding my so-called career, but I do regret the anxiety I caused Susan who was rightly concerned about our survival in the Middle East with the children, or subsequently in UK as I had no job to go back to.

After Parish Communion at St Mark's, Broomhill, we were given a fine send-off from our house in Sheffield and, facing a journey of over 7,000 miles driving, took a wrong turn at Mansfield and were late getting to Susan's parents at Newton, near Nottingham. They were very hospitable but mother-in-law also thought we were mad and taking quite unnecessary risks, particularly as the weather forecast for crossing the Channel next day was *'severe gale, force 9, rising to force 10 locally'*. Most of us were sick and, as seasickness makes one depressed, I wondered if we would ever see England again. But thereafter the weather and our spirits improved and there was some sun in the south of France.

When we stayed beside the sea for a few days we put up tents, but for overnight stops Susan and I slept on the settees each side of the table, Carole and Ruth in bunks above, and two more children in the 'luton', the space above the driver's cab. Peter, aged two, slept on the bench seat in the cab and when I got up early to drive, I pushed him along to the passenger's side and he slept on, just as the crowd in the back did too. Sometimes we would travel 100 miles before stopping for breakfast and the rest of the day. This way, the children did not get too fed up with being on the move and Carole was able to do some school work with them, sitting in a lay-by or on a camp site.   They posted reports back to their school in Sheffield, as instructed. We also used to sing songs to keep them occupied and we still do on family occasions, the favourite being *When I first came to this land,* which seemed a very appropriate title for our situation, for we travelled across nine countries.

We settled into a travelling mode and I soon forgot all about Sheffield and work but concentrated on the pleasures and logistical problems of travelling.   Ruth became our liturgical advisor and helped to lead the Sunday service, wherever we happened to be. She had found some bamboo palm leaves and distributed them to all of us, including two intrepid women from USA, motor caravanners voyaging with us on the ferry from Bari, on the Adriatic coast of Italy, to Corfu on Palm Sunday. From there we continued through Greece to the Bulgarian border where customs officials were nonplussed to see three little girls leaping about in their nighties. With the help of the phrase book, Susan explained that they should not search the caravan for contraband until Peter had finished sitting on his potty. They quickly agreed.

From Istanbul we crossed the Bosphorus on a chaotic ferry and at Konya, in the middle of Turkey, we had our only puncture of the journey and I had to fit a patch to the outer casing with a kit we had brought from UK. This was a popular event beside the road in the town centre, surrounded by a crowd of children, amazed at the sight of these strange western Europeans travelling in a vehicle the like of which they had never seen. On we went across the plateau and down to the Mediterranean at Silifke. There is a picture of Mary, aged 7, surrounded by a flock of sheep and one of Rebecca cleaning her teeth by the roadside. Peter, aged two, fossicked around the motor caravan which he regarded as home, and was oblivious of the location.

At Spear & Jackson, our works lorry driver was Bill who spent most of his life shovelling, loading and unloading. Always good humoured and ready to pause for a chat, his most treasured experiences, apart from shovelling which he enjoyed, was his war service with the local regiment, The Hallamshires. He had been an army driver and had ferried generals around the Middle East in a powerful staff car. As works manager I used to see Bill several times a week about some load or other and therefore I accumulated knowledge of his travels, huge and unexpected experiences for someone brought up in the back streets of Sheffield, with few expectations of travel beyond an annual day outing to Scarborough. When we were planning our journey I asked him if he had any advice from his knowledge of the roads in that area. After a little thought he said, '*Make sure you turn right at Aleppo.*' Seemingly there were two imperceptible roads out of Aleppo at that time and the wrong one would have taken us to Baghdad and Iran. In the event, we did not quite go to Aleppo but turned right rather sooner to take us down the coast to Lebanon. But '*turn right at Aleppo*' has passed into family jargon for giving simple and clear travel instructions.

We spent five days in Syria, visiting Crusader castles, shopping in Homs, to Damascus and then through Jordan down to Jericho and the Dead Sea where we swam and visited the cave where the scrolls were found in 1953. On 1 May 1967 we entered Jerusalem, 65 days out from Sheffield. At that time it was a divided city and when we presented ourselves at the Mandelbaum Gate to enter Israel, the customs official said :-

"*Where have you come from?* ". I replied, "*Jordan. Just over there.*" He said, "*We do not recognise Jordan; there is no such country.*" "*If you say so, but please may we come through your gate into Israel.*"

They allowed us through, reluctantly, and a few weeks later, after the Six Day War, Israel annexed the Jordanian sector of Jerusalem.

We spent a month exploring Israel and lived on a remarkable kibbutz in Galilee which, as well as growing bananas and lemons, included a factory making cutting tools which must have been an influence on me when, years later, we were founding members of a Christian residential community and I was involved for years in the formation of employee-owned co-operative businesses which are structurally similar to the kibbutz pattern. We left Israel on the last ship out of Haifa before war engulfed the country, and drove back from Venice via Switzerland to Taizé and thence home. We had been away for four months and travelled 9513 miles of which 7743 were by road and 1770 by sea. The total running cost, including food, petrol and camp sites, was £456 which was within the permitted foreign Travel Allowance of £150 per person. An unforgettable journey.

Since that journey we seem to have been inescapably drawn to visiting monasteries, mostly on islands or hill tops, like Taizé where we have stayed numerous times, Monte Oliveto in Tuscany, Our Lady of the Rock on Shaw Island,USA, Theologos in Greece, Bizen in Eritrea, as well as Iona closer to home. If we had known of monasteries on islands or hills in New Zealand or Israel, or Morocco, I guess we would have visited somehow or other.

L 'SHARING OUR INDUSTRIAL FUTURE' - 1967

Back in UK after our journey to Jerusalem I looked for work as chief executive of a medium-sized manufacturing company willing to be managed in a genuinely participative manner. I had the experience and all the qualifications but my ideas on shared decision-making were unacceptable. I went to Plymouth to consider being managing director of Fine Tubes Ltd., an offshoot of an American company making precision steel tubes for medical equipment, and found the workforce on strike and picketing the front entrance. *"Ignore the bastards"*, said the American director who was due to return to the US parent company and was therefore looking for a replacement, *"Don't even look at them"*. When I suggested it might be useful to listen to their case, he decided I was 'too soft' and the employment offer was withdrawn.

Both Susan and I enjoyed and benefited from being involved with groups such as the Sheffield Industrial Mission and St Mark's Church and the squash club. We had lots of friends, some of whom were mystified by my decision to leave Spear & Jackson, but gradually I left the Sheffield steel hierarchy and finally abandoned any previous ambition to be Master Cutler. I think Susan was relieved because she never saw herself as a Mistress Cutler opening bazaars, but some of our friends were disappointed as they would miss out on the coveted invitation to the Cutler's Feast, a prestigious annual event. I remain a Freeman for life but have had no active contact with The Cutler's Company for a good many years.

Instead, not finding a job of the kind I wanted, I accepted an invitation from John Garnett, Director of The Industrial

Society, to research companies with high levels of participation as this was currently regarded as an incoming change of culture from the traditional confrontational attitudes between formidable trade unions at a time of high employment and would-be dictatorial managers. The Industrial Society had set up a strong steering committee for the project, including Jim Conway, General Secretary of the Amalgamated Engineering Federation, a powerful Trade Union, and Adrian Cadbury, Chairman of Cadbury's.   It was chaired by Charles March (Earl of March, later Duke of Richmond) who was Director of Studies at William Temple College, Rugby, where I wrote the report after travelling all over the UK gathering information.

My report was completed in 1968 and was published by The Industrial Society under the title *Sharing Our Industrial Future.* It drew together the experience of some large firms such as ICI , Esso, Cadbury, and the John Lewis Partnership, together with smaller and more radical businesses. However its impact was limited because the steering group, shortly before the book went to press, decided that the companies described should be referred to by code letters, A,B,C etc. and not by their real names. There is a great difference between reading that 'Company A' was drawing more people into the decision-making process, and knowing that this company was ICI, a household name. The prestigious names on the steering committee were hesitant about being publicly associated with these tentative moves towards industrial democracy. Once again, I seemed to be on a more radical path than those around me.

M   TRYLON Ltd. 1968- 1975   (41-48)

I realised from my job hunting that a well-established company was unlikely to employ me as chief executive, despite my track record, and the only way to realise my concern to develop real employee participation was to start from scratch.

For some people, the striving for power and money gives satisfaction and, if successful, such people may become grasping bankers or ruthless top executives, but I had discovered long ago that contentment comes from friends and family and having a purpose, so it was no great sacrifice for me to forego the material benefits which the chief executive of a medium-sized company could expect. My ambition now lay in a different direction.

Help was at hand in the shape of Scott Bader Ltd, a medium-sized business making polyester resins for glassfibre construction, founded and developed by Ernest Bader, Swiss Quaker, pacifist, vegetarian. I had visited Scott Bader in Northamptonshire and included them, as 'Company F (350 employees, chemicals)' in *Sharing Our Industrial Future,* because Ernest Bader had recently completed the trans-formation of this thriving family firm into an employee-owned business.

Ernest, now in his 80's and supposedly retired, wanted to initiate another more radical experiment called Trylon, but the Scott Bader directors refused to lend him the starting capital because, they said, he was too old and why didn't he shut up and retire gracefully, basking in the sunshine of what he had achieved at Scott Bader. Ernest was furious and had no intention of basking in any sunshine, so when I arrived to write up the Scott Bader story, he proposed to the Board that Scott Bader should rent a nearby building to Trylon at a peppercorn rent if I was willing to come as managing director. The directors accepted this compromise, as it might get Ernest off their backs, and it was just the opportunity for which I was searching.

So, in April 1968 I started work at Trylon, near Northhampton, with the grand title of managing director. Those to be directed were Ron Munday, Sid Cleaver, a talented artist and Canaan Mutemasango, an asylum-seeker from South Africa. All three were former Scott Bader people whom Ernest Bader had invited to become a development group for the artistic use of polyester resins.

Our family, six of us, moved to Northampton in July and the only people we knew there were Michael and Dorothy Atkinson, from industrial mission days. Susan had little opportunity to make new contacts because of the demands of four small children, two at new schools and two at home round her feet. I was busy, working all hours, and not giving as much attention as I should to the family. Now and again, when we had a crisis at Trylon, which was quite often in the early years, I wondered if Aunt Isa had been right and I should have stayed in Sheffield and reaped the rewards that Spear & Jackson had offered. Maybe. We would have been 'comfortably off' and perhaps well regarded by top society in Sheffield, but I would have been frustrated and irritable, and Susan knew it. In Sheffield we had been a three-car family and, for a time in Northampton, we kept the motor caravan for holidays and Susan's stripey green mini but after a few years we reduced to one small van which also doubled as the Trylon delivery vehicle. I do not remember feeling deprived by these reductions but I do recollect a huge journey of 523 miles in a day, from Inverness to Northampton, returning from a half-term holiday in the very furthest northwest corner of Scotland with four of us squashed into a small car. We always seemed to be going further and stretching the limits more than our contemporaries.

The Trylon development group made table tops, pictures and paper weights from resin and showed what a versatile material it was. Sid Cleaver made a huge sculpture cross four metres high for the outside wall of Emmanuel Church, Northampton. We quoted for other sculptures but these projects were too uncertain as a basis for a business that needed to provide a livelihood for four people and we needed a more saleable product. We did some work on resin flooring which was poured as a viscous liquid and then set as a seamless level surface. This was attractive to the food industry where hygiene is a priority and we obtained an order from Weetabix at Burton Latimer to provide a floor in a large new production area. It was aquamarine blue and looked beautiful when we had laid it, just like a tropical sea on a flat calm day. Two weeks later when they were starting to install the production machinery, we had a phone call from an angry manager to say the floor was cracking. It certainly was, the bond with the underlying concrete had failed and sheets of brittle resin were coming loose and curling up to resemble a rough sea, more like the Southern Ocean than the tropics.

"*You'd better come and take the whole bloody thing away*", he said, so Canaan and I spent many hours shovelling up the floor, all of which had now come loose, into wheelbarrows and tipping it on the local dump. Not unreasonably, Weetabix declined to pay anything for this disaster and it proved to be Trylon's lowest moment as we were almost bankrupt within a few months of starting to trade. It was little consolation to learn that three out of five new businesses fail within the first two years. It was even less consoling, I thought as I shovelled, that I could have been sitting in a comfortable office in Sheffield with my secretary bringing coffee and biscuits.

Because Trylon was adjacent to Scott Bader, with their extensive knowledge of polyester resin technology, I heard about the possibilities of making fibreglass canoes, so, as we desperately needed an alternative product to the aborted flooring in order to keep the business alive, we turned to canoe building which proved to be a great success and was the backbone of Trylon for years to come. A number of companies were soon making these canoes but we deliberately went a step further back in the process and sold the moulds from which schools and youth clubs could make their own craft. We ran courses in canoe-building and sold the materials with the mould.

John Crane joined us as sales manager and became an indefatigable enthusiast, touring the country, delivering the moulds and teaching the canoe building process. Unlike many sales managers he often slept in the van overnight. We had hit upon a niche market as no one else was selling moulds and, in due course, John reckoned there were 30,000 Trylon Tiger canoes in use in UK, far more than any other design. A well-organised school craft group could build six canoes in a weekend and, of course, we sold the materials and equipment such as paddles and spraydecks.

Small is often beautiful and small is relative as we were truthfully able to advertise ourselves as the largest canoe mould makers in Europe.

For me the work at Trylon was a reflection, however dim and obscure, of the Christian faith which bound us together. Benedict had proclaimed in the 6th century that *'prayer is the work of the monastery'* and this is complemented by manual work. So *laborare est orare* and *orare est laborare.* Among this small group of co-operative pioneers, Ron Munday, who was a non-stipendiary Baptist minister, was the most committed to this concept that our work was a totally integral part of our faith journey. From time to time this made him an awkward colleague because others who joined us as the business grew, were less concerned with the Gospel, and regarded Ron as a religious fanatic and a killjoy. However, I was grateful for his strongly held views and when we came to write the Preamble, our mission statement, we agreed that our object was to express *'through our work our shared belief in the spiritual nature of man'.*

Ernest Bader, as a Quaker, had always seen a close connection between work and faith, but for a time he kept clear of Trylon, perhaps wondering whether it would survive. However, when he saw that the business was prospering, he began to take a much closer interest and decided that he should be nearer to the action. John Crane liked to introduce me to his sales contacts, many of whom had a high opinion of his ability, and on one occasion he asked me to go with him to a craft exhibition at Sussex University where he was delivering canoe moulds and materials. My recollection is that he would sleep in the back of the van surrounded by cans of resin, and I would have the luxury of the bench seat in the cab. Ernest, aged 83, heard I was going to be away for the weekend and without any consultation, called a board meeting at which he intended to claim that Trylon's growing success was too dependent on me and that he should be appointed managing director, in my place.

When I returned, it would be a fait accompli.   However, one of our trustees, Frank Scuffham, heard about Ernest's scheme and got a message to me in Sussex. We packed up early, drove back to Wollaston overnight and, to Ernest's surprise and annoyance, I appeared at the meeting and suggested that Ernest was a bit too old for the job. Despite his prestige, as founder of Scott Bader the working group backed me up and Ernest retired hurt. Such manoeuvres were typical of him, as a successful business man not wanting an opportunity to slip past him.

When we had a disagreement, which was not infrequent, Ernest sometimes drove ten miles in the middle of the night to deliver a fiery letter to me. Susan was understandably perturbed by this spontaneous combustion and dreaded being woken at 3am by the clang of the letter box. Nevertheless, we remained good friends and years later in 1981 his last outing, before he died aged 91, was to Daily Bread Co-operative to give us his blessing and warn us about some of the errors which he reckoned Scott Bader had made when he was no longer managing director. His story is told in *The Man who Gave his Company Away,* by Susanna Hoe (Heinemann 1978), with a significant Foreword by E.F.Schumacher who had published his seminal book *Small is Beautiful* a few years earlier. I had got to know Schumacher and have been much influenced by his ideas ever since those early Trylon days.

In due course, John Crane moved on and developed a substantial business. He told me, years later, that his experience at Trylon had been hugely important to him in learning entrepreneurial skills.

Trylon continued to grow and within a few years we had repaid the starting loan and had no debts. I wrote, ' *No intrinsic merit is seen in growing large and a group of around 25 people may be the best size to combine the objectives of providing a high level of security and a reasonable standard of living for Members, together with a concern for the quality of life at work, and an outgoing concern for others'.*

By 1974, after six years, I considered my work was done and left in August to become self-employed, concerned with developing employee-ownership on a national scale. I continued as a Trustee until 1996, a total of 28 years involvement. Michael Angerson, a Quaker from Bristol, was appointed manager and stayed for over twenty years. At the time of writing (2016), Trylon continues as a small business supplying craft materials to schools and craft shops, democratically owned and controlled by the working members.

N   SELF-EMPLOYED 1974- 1980   (47-53)

After leaving Trylon in 1974 I decided not to look for another job within the worker co-operative sector but to work from home for the time being, from a desk in our bedroom.

The 1970's was an exciting time for those of us trying to forge a new way of working together, concerned with the quality of life at work as well as the necessity of keeping the bottom line black rather than red.   The John Lewis Partnership was becoming known as a major exponent of employee-ownership but their history and constitution was complex and did not provide a model for small new businesses to follow.   They tended to be rather aloof from the grassroots movement.

Scott Bader had been owned by employees for ten years and some of their leaders were keen to spread the word and were very helpful to new starters who knocked on their door, giving advice and sometimes making generous loans as working capital.

However, in the same way that the John Lewis Partnership was dominated by Spedan Lewis, so too Scott Bader was dominated by its founder, Ernest Bader, and he wanted every new employee-owned business to be committed to pacifism, vegetarianism and a few more 'isms' which were not necessarily the concern of these new groups.   Nevertheless, there was enthusiasm for industrial democracy and need for an organisation bring the enthusiasts together. As initiators of unconventional ways of working together, we were inevitably a group of mavericks and found it difficult to agree on a descriptive title for the organisation. Some wanted it to be a 'commonwealth', others including me, pleaded that it was no more and no less than a resurgence of the development of the co-operative movement in the 19th century and why did we not simply join up with this? However, at that time, many retail local co-operatives were in decline, challenged by Tesco and Sainsbury's, and it was considered that we should not attach ourselves to 'the Co-op' which seemed to be an ailing giant.

We decided on the descriptive phrase 'common ownership' but, right from the start, this was to be a misleading title, particularly as the famous Clause IV of the Constitution of the Labour Party, printed on every membership card, used the phrase to describe nationalisation which is entirely different from employee-ownership :-

> *'To secure for the workers by hand or brain the full fruits*
> *of their industry and the most equitable distribution thereof*
> *that may be possible upon the basis of the common ownership*
> *of the means of production, distribution and exchange ...'*

After much informal discussion about titles, the Industrial Common Ownership Movement (ICOM) was initiated at Scott Bader's premises at Wollaston near Northampton in 1971. Their meeting room was capacious, with a remarkable parabolic roof, and a huge painting entitled *The Platform Party*, showing a group of politicians, bankers and judges, discussing what was 'best' for the mass of ordinary people, grouped below the platform and thus prohibited from participating in the debate.

The founder members of ICOM were a disparate bunch of unconventional businesses, influenced by a corresponding group of unconventional entrepreneurs.   Scott Bader with 400 employee-owners and highly respected in the chemical industry, was the largest and most well-established having been transferred to employee-ownership during the 1960's. In size, it was closely followed by Bewley's Cafes, based in Dublin, also with about 400 employee-owners.   The other early members were an assorted collection of small businesses in fields as widely dispersed as glassfibre canoes and portable loos. An unusual member was Fakenham Enterprises, a group of feisty women in rural Norfolk who achieved national fame on TV by organising a 'sit-in' when their employer threatened to make them redundant.   The 21 'Ladies of Fakenham', as they became known, decided to go it alone and, with help from Scott Bader, formed themselves into a women's co-operative, although, as they declared, ' *occasional males are used as part-time accountants..... and in other menial capacities* '.

The first edition of *This is ICOM - a description of the Industrial Common ownership Movement* in 1974 lists ten employee-owned businesses. Trylon is described as 'a group of 20 people with a turnover of £250,000 '. The fourth and last edition, in 1980, has over 200 entries. Thereafter the directory was compiled by the national Co-operative Development Agency (CDA) and the Co-operative Research Unit (CRU) at The Open University.

Having left Trylon and become self-employed, I threw myself into this development work, in due course being elected Chairman of ICOM and earning an exiguous living from advising groups wanting to start employee-owned businesses. It was during these years that the house communion group came into being in the parish of Weston Favell where we lived. This was a group of nine people which started as a conventional Lent group but continued with a life of its own for over ten years until four of us moved house to become the initial members of

The Neighbours Community . The story is told in the next section and, at length, in my book *Under One Roof*.

One problem for incipient co-operatives was the provision of working capital. High street banks have a policy of demanding the house deeds of the founders of new businesses as security against loans and, not surprisingly, employee-members of emerging co-operatives were reluctant to put their houses on the line as well as their jobs. So, at a meeting in our living room in Northampton, we formed Industrial Common Ownership Finance (ICOF), as a revolving loan fund, taking in loans from well-established organisations such as Scott Bader and lending to new start-ups and conversions.

As I had the time and energy to offer, I became the administrator of ICOF, starting with a handful of incoming loans from well-wishers *

* Forty years on, in 2016, under the trading name, Co-operative and Community Finance, ICOF lends over £1 million a year to a variety of co-operatives and socially-concerned businesses. It is regulated by the Financial Services Authority (FSA) and is *'the oldest community development finance institution (CDFI) in the UK'*.

After a few years we appointed a full-time administrator for ICOF, Norman Lowe, and I was elected Chairman . It was the time that the Labour Party was being torn apart by the hard left 'militant tendency' and ICOF was targeted by a group of such militants who narrowly failed, at an emotionally charged AGM, to take over the organisation. I do not know what they would have done with it.

Co-operatives became a national issue in 1973 when Triumph motor bikes ran into financial trouble and looked likely to close.

Together with two other substantial businesses, also hit by the recession of the 1970's, the Triumph workers decided to reject redundancy and formed themselves into Meriden Workers' Co-operative. They looked for political support and appealed to the government to give them financial backing. Tony Benn was the Labour government Minister involved and he agreed and made substantial loans to all three businesses to keep them afloat as worker co-operatives.

However, there was very little experience of co-operative structures for medium-size or large businesses and the workers' representatives had almost no business background with the result that none of the three survived as co-operatives, Meriden being the last to close in 1983. Conservatives reacted gleefully to this failure with undisguised schadenfreude and the media piled-in to declare that employees were incapable of management and should leave it in the hands of professional managers. This was strange because it was these same professional managers who had led these companies into near-bankruptcy in the first place. But, arguing from the particular to the general, the press persuaded politicians and the public that no co-operatives could work effectively.

This debacle set back the public perception of employee-ownership for at least 25 years. The truth was more complex than politicians or newspapers were prepared to admit; certainly it was a fact that the co-operators elected to be directors had little or no experience but it was also a fact that these businesses were beyond repair by professional managers or co-operators. The shareholders escaped with the government bail-out but most of the employees lost their jobs in due course.

The failure of the Benn co-operatives delayed the acceptance of employee-ownership for a whole generation. Tony Benn, with the best intentions, had been badly advised by civil servants; it would have been better to put government support behind small co-operative businesses to establish a solid base of good practice and build up the co-operative sector organically and slowly, rather than jump into the deep end with comparatively large nationally-known companies like Triumph

ICOF was a sister organisation of ICOM and both were weakened by the Benn failures, but did not despair and continued to make the case for employee-ownership. In 1975 David Watkins, MP for Consett, won a high place in the annual ballot for private Members' Bills and therefore had a good chance of success. Moreover he had already sponsored a Bill which had become the Employer's Liability (Compulsory Insurance) Act 1969 and knew a great deal about the tortuous task of getting a Private Members' Bill onto the statute book. We knew he had been involved with resisting the closure of Consett steel works, a dominant employer in his constituency, and we asked him to help us. He responded enthusiastically and I had the task of preparing a draft for what eventually became the Industrial Common Ownership Act 1976.

The parliamentary lawyers modified every sentence of my draft in order to put it into legal jargon, so what could have been a simple piece of legislation became complex and difficult for most people to understand. However, Lord Melchett (who later resigned his peerage to become straightforward Peter Melchett) made a brilliant speech in the House of Lords and the Bill squeezed through on the last day of the parliamentary session and received the Royal Assent on 22 November 1976. Peter had concluded his speech by saying that we would look back on equity share companies, concerned with benefits for remote shareholders, in the same manner that we now regarded conditions of employment in Victorian times, when children were allowed to work in coal mines. "*In a democratic country*" , he said, "*we take it for granted that Members of Parliament are elected by citizens, so it would be regarded as very odd that people earning their livelihood in a business enterprise had no say in management.*"

ICOM held a reception at the House of Commons to celebrate the Act and to pay tribute to David Watkins' skill and determination to get it through. I said that the only similar campaign I could trace was the Industrial & Provident Societies Act of 1856, a historic piece of co-operative legislation, which was sponsored by the Christian Socialists and specifically by F. D. Maurice who went on to be Professor of Theology at King's College, London. David's secretary muttered, "*Frankly, I don't see him becoming a professor of anything*", and David then made it clear that he had no theological or ecclesiastical ambitions.

Only a few employee-owned businesses registered under the terms of the ICO Act but it put some Government money behind ICOF and was excellent publicity for industrial co-operatives. As chairman of ICOM and ICOF I found myself involved in discussions with civil servants and Ministers about ways in which the government could support democratic industrial enterprises. I was amazed at the hierarchical structure of the civil service; only the senior civil servant spoke at meetings unless he asked one of his juniors to make a comment.

We invited Tony Benn to speak at the ICOM AGM in London in 1976. He spied reporters at the back of the room and so he placed a tape recorder in a prominent position on the table in front of him, telling me, chairing the meeting, that he was often misquoted and needed to make sure his speech was recorded to avoid misrepresentation. He gave a spirited declaration of support for worker co-operatives but I noticed afterwards that the tape recorder was not switched on. "*I know*", he said, "*I don't usually switch it on. Too expensive in batteries*".

The historical co-operative movement, based in Manchester, was dominated by the high street retail co-operative stores which had serious problems of their own and they hardly took part in the 1970's debates about employee ownership. Most businesses are incorporated under the Companies Acts and governed by the Memorandum and Articles of Association under which the Members own and control the Company. There is no mention of the employees in these Acts and the assumption is that the Members are the shareholders who provide the working capital. The early co-operators in the 1850's had broken away from this ownership concept and adopted the Industrial and Provident Society Acts (IPSA), under which co-operatives registered with Rules. Over a century, as circumstances changed for retail co-operatives, such Rules had been added-to but seldom subtracted-from, so they had become unwieldy and almost impossible for lay people to grasp. Some ran to over 100 pages of legalistic text and were totally unsuitable for new employee-owned businesses. So, on behalf of ICOM, I undertook the task of drafting a simple set of updated Model Rules, which could be registered quickly and inexpensively. The objective was to have them 'on one sheet of paper' instead of 100.

To test out the procedure for these new Rules in 1976 I asked a group of friends, members of the Christian house group attached to our local parish church in Northampton, to become the required seven founder members of a proposed employee-owned co-operative business and suggested we call it Daily Bread Co-operative Ltd. At this stage we had no immediate plan to initiate a trading business. These Rules seemed to be what was needed and I wrote-up the procedure for forming a new co-operative business in what became known as the ICOM Green Book .   The Rules were adopted by many new co-operative businesses and by 1977 there were over a hundred ICOM member firms accepting the stated Object, ' *To achieve democratic control of their own work by people at work* '.

A few years later, when I felt the need to return to direct involvement rather than consultancy, we were able to use the Rules to start a new trading business, Daily Bread Co-operative Ltd. Maurice Walton designed a 'loaf ' logo and both this and the Rules have continued unchanged for over forty years, allowing the co-operative members to get on with the task of building the business rather than an endless debate about constitutional details which has bogged down some ground-breaking enterprises. Entrepreneurs in this field are often re-inventing the wheel.

The 1976 Model Rules have since been refined and there are now (2016) several different versions administered by Co-operativesUK. Registration is not difficult.   Looking back, I think the work of developing these Rules in the 1970's was the most useful task of my self-employed years.

P   NATIONAL CO-OPERATIVE DEVELOPMENT AGENCY
1978 - 1980   (51-53)

The secretary of ICOM, Manuela Sykes, was a persistent lobbyist for employee ownership and in due course this led to much more parliamentary interest and to the Co-operative Development Agency (CDA) Act in 1978, which initiated the national organisation under the chairmanship of Bert Oram, a seasoned campaigner for co-operatives, now in the House of Lords. I served for two years as a board member of the CDA which soon decided to focus on worker co-operatives. Several sets of Model Rules were prepared and new co-operative ventures began to proliferate. The *Directory of Industrial & Service Co-operatives*, published by the CDA in 1980, listed 330 employee-owned businesses and the 3rd. Edition in 1984 showed 911. I was asked to write a Foreword to this edition and claimed that the movement towards employee ownership 'had come of age'. Certainly the number kept growing, reaching a high water mark of 1400 co-operatives in the last edition of the *Directory,* published by the Co-operative Research Unit (CRU) at the Open University in 1989.

However, by then, the national CDA was influenced by new board members appointed by the Conservative government and had changed direction, away from businesses owned by their employees and towards limited employee share ownership and '*promoting the development of participation by employees*'.
Very laudable but inevitably and deliberately diluting the former message. In vain E.F.Schumacher, the author of *Small is Beautiful* , affirmed the wholly employee-owned chemical manufacturer, Scott Bader, and declared that '*until you have changed ownership you have changed nothing*'.

The government responded by closing the CDA in 1990, with mellifluous words and 'gongs' for the chairman and director. It has not been resuscitated. A miserable end to a project which started with high hopes of underpinning a significant sector of the economy, but lost its way

Not surprisingly, anxious to maintain control by the owners of capital, real democracy in the workplace was ignored by the Conservative governments of the 1980's and 1990's.*

 * Much more surprising and sad, co-operatives were also largely ignored by the ensuing Labour governments from 1997 which put their faith and their money into the absentee equity share market and high risk bank loans, a policy which led to the financial crisis of 2008. The enthusiasm built up in the 1970's had evaporated and the number of worker co-operatives dwindled back to 403, recorded by Co-operativesUK in the annual *Co-operative Review 2008.*

At a meeting about co-operatives in the 1980's I found myself sitting next to Jo Grimond who had been Leader of the Liberal Party between 1953 and 1967. He had been translated to the House of Lords. I congratulated him but he replied, " *Don't let them put you in the Lords, Sawtell, it's political suicide".* I do not think there was ever much risk that *they* would put me anywhere, let alone the House of Lords.

However, my ICOM/ICOF work took me to the House of Lords from time to time and I began to find my way about the maze of corridors and meeting rooms which make up the Palace of Westminster, often meeting elderly peers shuffling along the corridors. One such was Ted Sorenson with an enviable record of public service as Labour MP for Walthamstow. He was now a life peer. Driving with him from Westminster to his home in east London, ignoring the traffic pounding round him, he parked on a double yellow line in Tavistock Square (possibly a privilege of the peerage, for no policeman disturbed him) to show me the statue of Gandhi in the middle of the square. He told me it had taken him 20 years to put this memorial in place and he regarded it as the most useful thing he had done in his life, more so than any of his parliamentary work. Tavistock Square was the site of one of the London bombings on 7 July 2005, a horrible irony as Gandhi is perhaps the most widely-known advocate of non-violent protest.

Many are now realising that we cannot go back to the kind of mad 'casino' banking and short term greed which precipitated the crisis in 2008 and co-operation is seen as a viable alternative business structure.   The number of employee-owned co-operative businesses has begun to increase again, and these businesses are on a much sounder footing due to experience gained from earlier years.   The future now looks bright but it has been a roller coaster ride and politics never stands still. If the ICOM founder members had joined the traditional co-operative movement in 1971, instead starting a new organisation, the employee-owned co-operative sector would be much more significant to-day.

I enjoyed this political involvement in the 1970's and even thought I might continue as a lobbyist for employee-owned co-operatives, or possibly stand for parliament, with the family precedent of Susan's father who had been a Labour MP for a short time in the 1930's and, for many years held the record for the smallest parliamentary majority, three votes. However, in the same manner as my father-in-law returned to the Bar rather than stay in politics, I began to feel that my call was to return to front line management rather than advisory work. A friend was fond of quoting the proverb, *'A consultant is a person who borrows your watch in order to tell you the time.'* So, responding to this guidance, my career took another sharp turn and I set about the task of turning Daily Bread Co-operative into a test bed for democracy at work. We opened for business on 1 October 1980; takings for the first week were £46.

Q   THE FAMILY GROWS UP - 1970's

Looking back at those self-employed years, from forty years on, I wonder how we survived financially as a family. My earnings were minimal, Susan had returned to work as an Occupational Therapist in the NHS but only part-time, so I think we must have been living on the cushion of savings from the Spear & Jackson years. I do not recollect any hardship but, of course, the children assured us that all their friends received more pocket money and I countered by telling them that most parents reported the same complaints and they could not all be right. All four were teenagers in the 1970's and involved in projects and pastimes that involved expenditure.

Amazingly, and partly because my earnings were insignificant, we never paid a penny towards school or university fees for any of them. I doubt if such generous state education will ever return and some of our grandchildren are saddled with substantial debts before they even start earning.   The only time we considered paying fees was to offer our son, Peter, the opportunity to go to Bedale's, a liberal private school in Sussex, for his 6th form years, to develop his musical ability. Bedale's had a national reputation for music teaching but Peter turned it down as being "*too risky*" by which he meant that he might lose touch with his friendship group in Northampton.

Ruth (born 1958) got a holiday job at Levi's, famous for jeans, to pay for travels to folk concerts. She did a geography degree at University College, London (UCL) and despite her forebodings that she had 'done very badly' in her finals, she came out with a good 2:1 and was awarded the Meyer Prize in 1980 for an essay on 'The Toba-Bataks', a remote tribe in

Sumatra which she had visited. She made a start on a post-graduate project about this tribe but decided not to continue with it and joined the NatWest Bank, choosing it in preference to the other banks because it was the only one with a woman on the Board. Being a good organiser and happy with figures, she progressed up the management scale and might have added to the number of women directors but met and married Nigel in 1988. They went to live in Haringey where their three children were born and later moved to St.Albans. Nigel also forsook banking in due course and has become an authority on employee-ownership.

Mary (born 1960) was a member of the Midlands gymnastics squad, one of the regional groups from which the Olympic Games team was recruited, and we took her to innumerable training sessions.   After leaving school she went to The University of the South Bank (London) and achieved a First Class degree in Nursing Studies.   Later she qualified as a health visitor working in the London docks area where life was tough. In 1985 she took time out to volunteer with Save the Children at a refugee camp in Sudan and I joined her there for a few weeks and we travelled north and camped out at the secret airstrip on the Red Sea from which some of the Falasha Jews from Ethiopia had been airlifted to Israel between 1977 and 1984. Mary and Tom also have three children and in due course moved from Brixton to Saffron Walden from where she works as a social researcher as well as continuing with health visiting. In 2002 The Maternity Alliance published her report *Lives on Hold – Homeless families in temporary accommodation.*

Rebecca (born 1963) often took the dog out before school and on one occasion, walking with her friends, she was too embarrassed to acknowledge me as I set off for work wearing my woolly hat. "*Why can't you be a solicitor or a bank manager, Dad, like most of my friends' dads* ", she said. She has a degree in Psychology from Brunel University where she met Denis. They went to work in Dumfries where they were married in 1995 and both have worked ever since as psychologists in the NHS with all its ups and downs. She also works as an Expert Witness in family court cases. She has had to cope with serious health problems which might have defeated a less robust person. Having been told that it was very unlikely that she could ever have children, they were delighted when Keir was born. The consultant gynaecologist said he could hardly believe there was room for a baby, due to the operations she had had to undergo. Eleanor was born a year or two later. They live near Leicester.

Peter (born 1964) showed an aptitude for music and was soon playing the French horn at the local music school and in the Northamptonshire County Youth Orchestra. He also played guitar in the pop group he formed with school friends, *Reluctant Heroes,* and has been involved with various music groups ever since. He went to Reading University, "*because the campus has a good outlook and plenty of trees",* and has a degree in Electronic Engineering. He worked at Broadcasting House for some years, sometimes 'squatting' on the top floor where the sound effects are stored, sleeping beside machines for simulating the sound of horses hooves. When the BBC decided to outsource his department, responsible for designing and installing radio recording studios, he moved to Seattle to do similar work in local radio. He and Reanna continue to live in Seattle where Susan and I have visited them several times, and explored the islands of Puget Sound.

During their childhood and teenage years we had a variety of wonderful summer holidays, caravanning and camping in northwest Scotland and in France around the beaches of Brittany and the Atlantic coast. Susan remembers that one of the few occasions she saw me rattled was when we all climbed the spiral staircase of an old lighthouse near Bordeaux. There was an ancient handrail on the wall side but none on the inside so we were at risk of falling into the abyss. The French seemed to consider this quite normal so we tried to keep a stiff upper lip like true Brits. I would not care to repeat the experience.

Our children have been a huge joy and blessing to us and Susan has no regrets about devoting many years to raising them. My contribution was more marginal and sometimes I felt I was too involved with my work and not enough with the family. Moreover, it is not as though I was earning much to keep them in a style to which they might have aspired and I am thankful that they do not appear to hold it against me in latter years.

In due course, grandchildren arrived; Helen 1989, Anna 1992, Sam 1994, Keir 1995, Joe 1995, Eleanor 1997, Ella 1998, and Louis 2000. Words can hardly describe the pleasure they have given us both as we have watched them grow from infants to children to teenagers and then to young adults. Of course,we had enjoyed the same developments with our children but as grandparents, one step away from the action, we can observe without being directly involved. What a privilege !

A NEW THING

THE STORY OF DAILY BREAD CO-OPERATIVE
1975-1985

JAMIE WALLACE

A NEW THING – the first ten years of Daily Bread
Co-operative. 1975-1985.

Susan at Theologos Monastery, Amorgos.   1994

Sister Tommy at Afabet, Eritrea,where National Friendship
Fund helped to restore a vital well.   1996

Breakfast at Keren, Eritrea.   2004

Family gathering. Northampton 2007

Mary, Ruth, Rebecca, Peter. Our golden wedding party 2007

Family at our golden wedding party.   2007
At the Neighbours Community, Ardington Road, Northampton.

R DAILY BREAD CO-OPERATIVE 1980-1996 (53-69)

F.D.Maurice, (1805-72), professor of theology at King's College, London, and chaplain at Lincoln's Inn, is regarded as the founder of Christian Socialism :-

' *In 1849 a working class socialist called Walter Cooper.. asked Maurice and Ludlow whether the Christian socialists would sponsor 'co-operative associations' which would be small workshops run on co-operative lines. They jumped at the idea, seeing it as an opportunity to put their ideas into practice. Maurice wrote, 'It is the special vocation of the Church in this age... to help and teach men to work together for the supply of their own necessities, and those of others, and to pray together.' Thus in February 1850 the Working Tailors Association was set up, followed by seven other co-operatives for different trades. In addition, a society was established to give advice and make loans to groups of workers who wanted to form co-operatives. Maurice kept in close touch with the associations and had no illusions about the difficulties that would be experienced as men who until then had been working for a wage learned to manage their own affairs together.'*

(*Island Vision* , Robert Van de Weyer 1988)

Reading about F.D.Maurice and other pioneers encouraged me to '*jump at the idea*' of starting a new co-operative as part of a '*special vocation of the Church*' in 1980, just as it had been in 1850, so Daily Bread Co-operative was born. (see Appendix I) This new business adventure was a long time in the planning. As well as the necessity to break even or make a surplus, it was to have several non-financial objectives such as providing work for people recovering from mental illness, selling ethically-sourced products and seeking to provide a quality of working life which was not noticeably present in the work experience of most of us heretofore.

Matthew 13:44 (NRSV) reads '*The Kingdom of heaven is like a merchant in search of fine pearls; on finding one pearl of great value, he went and sold all that he had and bought it.*'

Daily Bread was intended to be '*a pearl of great value*' but I realised that the merchant must have had a great deal of experience of fine pearls in order to recognise this particular one. An inexperienced merchant was unlikely to be able to tell the difference. A number of employee-owned co-operative businesses, initiated by enthusiastic young people, failed in the in the 1970's due to management inexperience and I realised that my role was to be the experienced *'merchant'* and the *'pearl'* was the challenge of forming an unconventional business. Having examined the option of transforming an existing company and finding it impractical in the business culture of that time, this pearl would have to be a new business and therefore small.

When most pundits were pontificating that it was essential to be a large business to survive in a market economy, I noted that many mergers, claiming to be 'for economies of scale', did not achieve such economies. They were more likely to be driven by the ambition of the directors, to eliminate a competitor and increase their own power and glory. Taking an alternative view, I had been encouraged by E.F.Schumacher who published his seminal book, *Small is Beautiful,* in 1973. He gave it the sub-title '*a study of economics as if people mattered* 'and included a chapter about employee-ownership.   He died unexpectedly in 1977 and I was invited,at short notice,to take his place to give a keynote lecture in India to The Trusteeship Foundation, a

Gandhian organisation based in Mumbai. I made good use of this opportunity to develop the concept of employee-ownership and sharpen-up my thinking. I noted a quote from Schumacher, '*Any intelligent fool can make things bigger, more complex and more violent. It takes a genius – and a lot of courage – to move in the opposite direction.*' I knew I was no genius and was not sure if I had enough courage to move in the opposite direction.

Sometimes the significant turning points in our lives do not become apparent until years after the events themselves, and sometimes such turning points are very apparent at the time. This one was the latter. The registered Rules of Daily Bread Co-operative had lain dormant since its registration as a co-operative society in 1976 but, on returning from India, I was determined to bring it to life as a small trading business.

As I pondered and discussed the possibilities with others, it dawned on me that all my previous work in industry, two years at English Electric, sixteen at Spear & Jackson, six at Trylon, were no more or less than preparation for this new task which was likely to be more demanding than any of them. I saw the huge opportunity to initiate Daily Bread Co-operative as an alternative form of business, concerned with issues of justice and quality of life at work, which could be a pattern for others to follow in due course. In 1980 I was 53, old enough to have gained considerable life experience but young enough to have the necessary energy to get a counter-cultural project off the ground. In 1980 the Conservative government was backing big businesses owned by remote shareholders and also private businesses owned by individual entrepreneurs. In both cases the rich were getting richer and the gap between rich and poor was widening. I was convinced that this was an unstable situation and would lead to a financial crisis. At the same time I was painfully aware of the fate of the large Benn co-operatives, so Daily Bread would need to be small and compact if it was to be a pattern for others to follow, after the expected crisis. It seemed an awesome task and I did not tell many others of this call. I felt a sense of destiny and had spent many years of preparation without realising for what I was preparing.

Preparing for the task

First I needed to strengthen myself, body, mind and spirit. Our family situation was changing as the two older girls were away at university and the younger two children were reaching the end of their school years, so the time-consuming load of ferrying teenagers here and there which Susan, more than me, had been carrying for years, was easing. She was comfortable in her work as an Occupational Therapist and would soon install a huge loom at home as we now had a spare room, and begin twenty years of weaving wonderful rugs and wall-hangings. As always, she supported my decision to return to paid work instead of self-employment. The pay was likely to be modest and, unlike the entrepreneurs of most successful conventional businesses, I would have nothing to sell to finance a pension, however 'successful' Daily Bread might become. However, it was not as risky for family finances as the previous move when I left Spear & Jackson with no job to go to and four small children to look after.

To free up more time I resigned as a magistrate after seventeen years and the Lord Chancellor wrote a kind letter of thanks but pointed out that as I was only 53, I would normally have been expected to serve for a further seventeen years until retirement at seventy. *

* I remained on the Supplemental List but a few years later, on Easter Monday 1985, with several of our family, I was at RAF Molesworth protesting against the

siting of nuclear-armed missiles there. The Ministry of Defence claimed we were trespassing and defacing their fence by hanging placards on it, so some people were arrested. The following week I received a sharp phone call from the Chairman of the Bench telling me, with undeniable logic, that I could not be taking part in civil disobedience events and at the same time remain listed as a Magistrate, responsible for administering the Law ! I agreed, it was upside down, so I resigned again.

I decided to stop playing competitive squash after one last fling by taking part in the UK National Championships at Derby where I was soundly defeated by an Australian sheep farmer who had come over determined to win the Vintage section. He was eventually beaten by the legendary Hashim Khan, aged well over sixty, who did not even need to take off his spotless white track suit.   It was a privilege to play in the same competition as Hashim.

Ethos

Arising from our debates at the house communion group over a period of several years, it was clear that the new business should be indissolubly linked to the Christian faith. It would have been unrealistic to assume that everyone 'off the street' would accept the radical framework of a co-operative with social objectives.   In order to work together effectively pioneers need to have ideals in common and as Christians, striving towards the Kingdom, it would be a bond. Once the co-operative concept took root, the baton could be handed on to all manner of groups, Christian or not. In this sense it was to be a microcosm of the development of education and health care in the 19th. century, both of which were developed by Christian groups before they became mainstream . This was not to say that it would be a 'Christian business' because that phrase had no discernible meaning to me but it was to be a group of committed Christians working together.   This was fundamental, and needed to be more apparent than we had managed at Trylon in the 1970's. So I pondered and prayed.

Right from the start in October 1980, the initial working group decided to have corporate morning prayers during working time and a regular communion service in the community meeting room. Years later in 2005, one of the working members, John Kerr, estimated that such prayers had caused a 'loss' of 40,000 working hours over a period of twenty five years ! Perhaps it was a 'gain' rather than a loss. The practice remains unchanged in 2016.

Together with industrial chaplains in the Diocese of Peterborough I had drafted a liturgy for a communion service for small groups and in due course, Daily Bread published it under the title '*A Simple Communion*'. It sold ten thousand copies, the only significant sales of the numerous pamphlets and stuff I have written about work. Members were encouraged to invite the minister of their local church to preside at our communion service on a rota basis, and many did so, on the understanding that the service was inter-denominational, because, over the years, Daily Bread members came from a variety of churches, Anglican, Roman Catholic, Baptist, Methodist, Pentecostal, Quaker and independent.

On one occasion, the visiting minister, a Church of England priest, set out his chalice and plate for the bread and wine and said to me, "*I have not brought a purificator. Do you have one?*" I had no idea what he meant and wondered if a purificator was a person, to ensure purity. If so, it was unlikely that one could be found in a hurry, among our disparate working group. So, playing for time, I said to a colleague, who was also a Church of England member, "*Michael says he needs a purificator. Can we help?*" My colleague looked equally blank and reserved his position by saying he would ask around. He was soon back saying that no one had any idea what was wanted.

"Michael, we don't seem to have any purificators in the building. Should we send out for one or can you manage without?"

" Oh that's OK," he said, *" a tea towel will do."*

" Yes, of course. Why didn't I think of it earlier. No problem."

People

The Gospels make it very clear that Christians identify with those most in need, whether their poverty is financial, emotional or spiritual. There are two large psychiatric hospitals in Northampton, admitting patients from all over the country, and therefore a higher than average number of people in the town, discharged from hospital but cut-off from their former relationships and locality. Within the house communion group we had been concerned with people suffering from mental illness, the Cinderella of the National Health Service, Michael Jones was chairman of the local branch of MIND, the mental health charity, and most of us had friends who had been in hospital from time to time so we knew that finding work was a considerable difficulty for people with a history of mental illness. So here was a social task for the new business, to create opportunities for such people to return to a working routine and help them to get back to 'open employment'.

I had no idea how demanding this would be.

It goes without saying that the business is the people in it and particularly for a business like Daily Bread which adopted the motto *'People before profit'*. In the early days we were well aware that if we failed to make a surplus of any kind, the business would eventually fail and *'people'* would not benefit, but we intended to move away from the convention, enshrined in the Companies Acts, that the dominant object was to optimise profit or asset value. These Acts, which covered almost everyone working in UK, hardly mentioned employees. In legal terms 'people' were little more than a means of achieving the statutory object of benefiting the shareholders. Victorian industrialists had used the term 'hands' and nothing much had changed in this regard for a hundred years. Our intention as an employee-owned co-operative business would be to fuse together the employers and the employees who would be the same people and we quoted Schumacher's phrase:- *'Until you have changed ownership, you have changed nothing.'* Radical economists phrased the same concept in different words, *'in a conventional company, capital employs labour; in an employee-owned business, labour employs capital.'*

All the above high-flown oratory was to be channelled into the business by the first three working members ! I was the first employee/owner/member starting work on 1 July 1980 and was soon followed by Anne Jones and Bill Mills. Anne was passionate about the centrality of the Christian faith and was a member of the house communion group. She supported the co-operative structure and understood it well because her husband had transferred his family business, Michael Jones Jeweller, into a co-operative. She quickly learned about wholefood and, as a qualified teacher, she was soon giving talks to local groups and visitors to our warehouse building. Anne is a 'yes' person and an ideal colleague for a new venture where the tasks were diverse and there was no 'custom and practice' to rely upon.

Bill had recently retired as a warehouse supervisor in the motor trade and was happy to accept the co-operative structure and the concept of wholefood, both of which were new to him. When the Church of England Alternative Service Book was published in 1980, the first authorised revision of the Book of Common Prayer, Bill said he read it with joy and found it as exciting as a good novel.   Utterly loyal and dependable, Bill was an ideal person to look after the shelves and supervise the temporary workers, recovering from mental disabilities.

Pay

Salaries and salary differentials are, of course, matters of major importance to most people at work. However much some pioneers may ignore pay levels, many people are tied to mortgages, dependants and expectations. In my case, we were still cushioned by savings made during my Spear & Jackson years and we were never in financial difficulties although the children used to sigh, when some treat was not forthcoming, and regret that I seemed unable to earn lots of money whereas, they claimed, all their friends' parents were 'loaded'. In the planning stages, we had several debates at the house communion group about the ethics and practicalities of pay differentials. Michael Jones held that, co-operative or not, all pay should be at market rates, but others argued that Daily Bread was intended to be a business which would break new ground and we should not be afraid to be radical rather than just following current custom and practice. In the event, we agreed to pay the same rate to each working member and temporary worker, together with additional allowances for children or other dependants or special circumstances. There would be no higher rates for specific jobs or length of service. One benefit of this flat pay structure was that anyone could be expected to do any job which, for a small new business, is important; the person responsible for stock control was also unloading lorries and everyone was on the rota for the till. The downside was that we might not be able to find a competent manager unless we were prepared to pay a higher rate.

A standard salary was agreed each year by the members meeting and some were paid more or less than standard by request and only with the agreement of the meeting. For example, in 1985, by which time there were twelve working members, eight were paid standard, two asked for more than standard because they had significant numbers of dependent relatives, and two chose less than standard.

Over the years since those initial debates, there have been a number of different management structures, including joint managers and, on one occasion, a 'troika' of three managers, but usually just one. Throughout these changes, the initial fundamental concept of the same hourly rate for all working members, with an additional allowance for dependants, has remained in place for over thirty years, and with some variations, this 'flat pyramid' continues in 2016. It has had the effect of keeping the business small and flexible.

Temporary workers
The people we took on who were recovering from mental illness we called 'temporary workers' to accentuate the policy that Daily Bread was an intermediate stage before they moved on to whatever work they were accustomed to before their illness. In our naivety we reckoned that six months would be the kind of time scale before they were ready to leave. We were totally wrong and soon discovered that recovery was a much longer process and that some would never return to open employment. Nevertheless, during those first years a surprising number of the temporary workers said how much they had been helped by doing 'a proper paid job' rather than a subsidised make-work project. Much of the credit for this positive result was due to Bill Mills, co-ordinating the packing and stacking on the shop floor. Because of their sometimes bizarre behaviour, he found some of them irritating at times but he persevered

because they represented 'the poor' which his reading of the Gospels convinced him was part of our task.

I don't think we were overwhelmingly patronising because we all had to work together as a team to get the work done. However, we certainly underestimated the time it would take for people who had been enclosed in a psychiatric hospital to feel confident enough to return to their former work.

Fiona (not her real name) was in secure accommodation at the hospital because she had threatened a colleague with an axe. She was now on 'limited release' and available for work. She was an excellent co-operative worker and eventually left to get married. She never threatened the customers nor, to the best of my knowledge, has she ever taken an axe to her husband.

James returned to teaching after about six months at Daily Bread but, with the wisdom of hindsight, this was too soon and within months he was back in hospital. Graham had been in hospital for a year or so and after a few months at Daily Bread, he said he could not go back to being a solicitor without risking further illness. We encouraged him to apply for other jobs locally, but he was not successful and, in due course, he applied to be a permanent member of Daily Bread rather than a temporary worker. He was accepted and later became the company secretary, working steadily for years until retirement. He was the first temporary worker to make this transfer and a number of others have done so since. We soon realised the magnitude of the employment problems facing anyone with a mental health record and we also realised that Daily Bread was in this for the long haul.

Structure

By 1980 I had long been convinced that there must be a 'better way' of organising productive work in small groups than the conventional limited company, owned by its shareholders some of whom would be the controlling directors and others would be faraway folk who knew little of the business they owned and were solely interested in dividends and share value. I thought also, from my Spear & Jackson experience, that employees, better educated than at any previous time, would not stand for this injustice indefinitely and there would be a move towards different structures, particularly at any time of economic crisis. I thought a crash would surely come and therefore 1980 was a good time to gain experience of an alternative. It was this thinking that had caused us to register Daily Bread as a co-operative society in 1976, rather than an incorporated company, so in 1980 the structure was already on paper.

The crash did come in 2008 with the failure of Northern Rock and the banking disaster which was precipitated by ridiculous risks taken by executives motivated by greed. They were not restrained by their shareholders who looked for dividends and short term gains in share prices.

In 1980 the task was to work out what the co-operative Rules would mean in practice. Co-operative principles have been tried and tested since the Rochdale Pioneers in 1844 and, with numerous ups and downs, the seven principles still hold up: open membership, democratic control by members, sharing any surplus, financial independence, education, mutual help between co-operatives, concern for community (see Appendix II) In keeping to these Principles, it is unlikely that a business will fall into the hands of asset-strippers and so a co-operative is a good structure for the kind of long-lasting small business that we were envisaging.

In these early days every member was on the rota for serving on the till and therefore came face to face with the customers on whom the business depends.   Flexibility also meant that everyone was available when necessary to unload delivery lorries before we invested in a forklift truck.

The formal Rules of Daily Bread Co-operative Ltd., registered in 1976, have not been changed in any way for forty years (2016). These Rules are deliberately minimal so that current members have as much flexibility as possible to make decisions at the weekly meeting. This regular meeting of members is the only decision-making body of the business and therefore changes can be made without delay.

Product

My task in 1980 was to find a suitable product.   Maurice Walton, a member of the house communion group, had designed a logo in the shape of a loaf of bread and the obvious follow-up to the name we had chosen in 1976 would be to start a bakery. I spent a day working at a village bakery at Yardley Hastings and decided that baking was not the answer. If we were to provide employment for people recovering from mental illnesses we needed work which could be picked up quickly by people with a wide range of abilities.   I looked at bicycle maintenance and house clearance without enthusiasm, and then detected a niche for wholefood, as an alternative to the rapidly growing reach of the big supermarkets which were offering highly-processed pre-packaged food, stuffed with sodium glutamate to extend shelf life, to 'save the housewives time' and enable them more easily to go out to work. The huge publicity budgets of the supermarkets claimed that their products were good value but when I investigated the wholesale bulk prices of staples like rice, oats, and dried fruit, I soon realised that the processing and packaging and advertising were all expensive and there was room for an alternative by providing basic food with minimum processing and simple packaging.

I discussed this with a friend, a successful entrepreneur and he said, "*Don't go into food. Too competitive. A basketful of big fat cats are cutting out all the smaller businesses. They've got the future all sewn up.*" I spent a few days with a recently started wholefood warehouse business, Community Foods in north London, and then trusted my instinct that my friend was wrong and there was indeed a good market opportunity in Northampton and it would provide the kind of employment we needed. The demand for food might fluctuate a little with weather or recession but the market is always there, unlike some products which disappear completely. We would need to to find a niche and develop it.

My hunch was right and Daily Bread has stuck to its knitting for thirty five years. Weighing, mixing and packing work can be learned in a week. Our first temporary workers, recently discharged from hospital, included a teacher, a farm worker and a solicitor, all of whom soon became efficient Daily Bread workers. We coined the word 'tesbury' (combining Tesco with Sainsbury) as a shorthand for the supermarkets and set out to provide a totally different ambience as well as a different product. We bought a lorry load of oak fencing posts, redundant from a local estate and had them made into rugged racks in the sales area and we had straw baskets instead of wire supermarket trolleys. Sometimes I sprinkled cinnamon round the doorway and one day I noticed a friend walking round the selling area :-

" Can you find what you want", I asked.
*" Yes I can. I'm not buying anything to-day but this is my
lunch break and I just like walking round this place and
absorbing the atmosphere."*

Wholefood led us in due course into a wide range of organic
products and also into Fairtrade, both of which fitted
naturally into our philosophy. We spent little or nothing on
advertising and were happy to let the business grow slowly by
word of mouth, knowing that many new businesses failed by
trying to do too much too quickly. We found that appropriate
growth was not dictated by the market but more by the rate
at which we could absorb new people into an unusually close-
knit working group.   Shared decision-making and prayer are
not the experience of many people at work.

In 1980 we planned to develop muesli which was just becoming
known as a healthy breakfast food, more nutritious than the
toasties and crispies which were loaded with sugar and sold by
means of colourful pictures and endless competitions on their
cardboard boxes. Ours was a simple, uncooked mix, carefully
put together after trials by dozens of volunteers and packed in
a plain bag with a bright yellow label. The simplicity appealed
to a growing number of people in the 1980's and the business
was soundly based on it.   Another initial product was honey
which we bought in bulk from Australia, heated up in a water-
jacket and ran out into jars, mostly larger than the standard
jam jar. We were able to sell this at little more than half the
price that 'tesbury' were charging.

Democracy
The chairing of the weekly meeting was an important role and
we agreed that it should not be undertaken by the manager.
We had been reading the first chapter of Acts at morning

prayers and decided to choose the chairperson by lot, like the choosing of the disciple to replace Judas Iscariot. *'Then they prayed and ….the lot fell on Mathias (Acts 1:24).'* As we had plenty of pasta in stock, we used sticks of macaroni to make the decision and the lot fell upon Paul, the youngest member present. He made a good job of chairing the meeting and keeping the manager in order.

In March 1983 Central TV featured 'the sugar debate' at Daily Bread as part of a series called *Something Different.* Some members argued that we should not sell any sugar as it was unhealthy, others said we must sell what the customers want . After a fierce debate, it was agreed to compromise by selling only brown sugar, processed as little as possible, and not put any sugar in our own mixes such as muesli. The TV producer wanted to show that the decision was made collectively by all the worker members and not by a remote manager or committee.

Efficient buying was vital to our business and wherever possible we bought bulk supplies from the docks where they were unloaded. Sometimes there would be a phone call from the importer :-

" *Good morning, Mr.Sawtell, we have just unloaded 10 tonnes of Afghan raisins and I can put aside two tonnes for you at £345 a tonne on the quay."*

" *Oh, er, the price seems right. We are a co-operative business and I shall have to take it to our meeting next Thursday and get a decision."*

" *I am not concerned about whether you are a co-operative or a vicious dictatorship, Mr.Sawtell, but I shall have sold them all long before next Thursday, so please say yes or no."*

Thereafter, I was given limited authority to spend whatever necessary on products, without reference to the meeting, but any decisions about people, hiring or firing, must be referred to the meeting and not taken solely by the manager. This was a good compromise between business necessity and shared decision-making . Members were generally wise regarding people and had better knowledge of each other's strengths and weaknesses. It was also wise to restrain someone like me who, although genuinely committed to shared decisions, was also apt to take all decisions myself if not restrained. I had been used to having such untrammelled authority at Spear & Jackson.

To collect a load of peanut butter I went to Wales to visit our supplier. It was a warm day and the doors of the processing department were open. I noticed that there was a group of fat starlings sitting on the rim of the mixing machine. We changed suppliers but I wondered about some of our own health and safety practices. We wanted the packing area to be adjacent to the selling space so that customers could see the work being done and talk to the packers, but the factory inspector insisted we move it further away and he was not interested in 'transparency'. We resisted what we considered unnecessary bureaucracy but sometimes we had to yield.

At the AGM in 1982 we had seven working members and the non-working founder members were able to resign so that the business thereafter would be totally employee-owned and controlled. Maurice Walton, one of the founders, suggested that we should have some non-executive trustees, to act as advisors if requested and to check that the members were adhering to our principles set out in the Preamble. Because Christmas was approaching we decided to call them the Three Wise Persons, as there was to be no gender discrimination.

Some have been active and their involvement has been appreciated but it has not been easy to find people to fill this role.

Finance

Every new business needs starting capital, some more, some less, to prepare the premises, buy initial stocks and pay salaries until a customer base and income is secured. Every entrepreneur takes a risk in spending money which may not be repaid if the business fails. The important concept of limited liability, introduced in the Companies Act 1862, enabled the entrepreneur to avoid being held responsible for the debts of a failed business. However, there is a downside :-

> *'The consequences of the Companies Act of 1862 were perhaps greater than that of any single measure in parliamentary history. They completed the divorce between the Christian conscience and the economic practice of everyday life. They paganised the commercial community. Henceforward an astute man by adherence to legal rules which had nothing to do with morality could grow immensely rich by virtue of shuffling off his most elementary obligations to his fellows. He could not only grow rich by such means. He could grow immensely powerful.'*

English Saga, Arthur Bryant (Collins 1940) p.215

In 1980 we looked back at a century of the Companies Act. It had certainly brought prosperity but at the cost of *paganising* the commercial community and there had been much *shuffling-off* of obligations. As a group of Christians we wanted to do our bit in searching for a Gospel-based structure for group working and the co-operative alternative seemed a more acceptable pattern.   I was determined not to load the initial members with debt and not to rely on shuffling-off our obligations if the business failed. It followed that we wanted to minimise the starting capital and discussing these problems with a friend, Neil Wates, who had been managing director of Wates Builders. He came up with an offer of a loan of £20,000 from Commonwork Enterprises, a trust he had initiated which supported alternative ways of working together.   With this help, it was not necessary for any of the founder members to put their money into the business, which was just as well as we did not have much to offer.

Aware of our obligation to this generous lender, I was keen to minimise capital expenditure, even to the extent of being parsimonious.   In the first year it was not unusual for the whole working group to be unloading a delivery truck, humping sacks of rice into the packing area and sometimes forming a chain to pass boxes of dried fruit from hand to hand to stack it in the warehouse.   Soon we relented and bought a pallet truck and a year or two later we installed a goods lift and got a forklift truck. My back benefited from these aids but we lost a fraction of the togetherness of working as a group on a major manual task.

Most of the delivery drivers probably thought we were quite mad, but some suppliers such as SUMA were also co-operatives and joined in the unloading task.   As SUMA prospered, they purchased a large articulated truck which squeezed into our yard with some difficulty. Like our policy on the till, all SUMA members were on the driving rota and this one knocked down our gate post with her back end as she drove out. The vehicle was so large and the driver was so far from the back that she did not realise she had hit anything and drove happily back to Halifax. We said nothing, but widened the gateway.

After the first three months trading in 1980 we had made a surplus of £26 but three years later we were able to repay the Commonwork loan in full. Sadly, Neil Wates had died of cancer and never saw the result of his risky starting loan.

The policy was to make a modest surplus each year and the business has achieved this for nearly every year since 1980. One or two loss-making years were financially negligible and soon rectified. Recently I asked the treasurer if Daily Bread had an overdraft or any outstanding loans. He was shocked and indignant at the question. *"We never have an overdraft"*, he said, with pride. Such financial independence has been of great value. The conventional assumption, of course, is that a business must borrow and grow to survive, but the Daily Bread ethos has always been to remain small and encourage others to initiate similar employee-owned co-operatives so that the co-operative sector gradually becomes a larger part of the economy.

Whenever a new working member was accepted, we had a ceremony at the weekly meeting for him/her to hand over a one pound coin as a formal Membership Share . Apart from this no Daily Bread members have ever made investments in the business and correspondingly, no one takes anything out when they leave.   The commitment is in terms of work, not money.

Most customers paid cash and it was years before Daily Bread accepted credit cards because we did not want to pay the 2% premium to the credit card company. We had to yield in due course. During the first few vital years we had no safe and I used to count the day's takings and stuff the notes into my back pocket, walk home across the golf course and put them under my pillow. One bedtime in midwinter there were almost no notes in my pocket and I realised that they must have fallen out of my pocket on my way home. I set out with a torch and found them scattered over the golf course, untouched by golfers as it was pitch dark or by inquisitive squirrels. Fortunately it was a calm dry evening with no wind and I found every one of them. I cannot remember if I admitted this embarrassing carelessness to my colleagues but I do remember recommending that we install a small underfloor safe, hidden behind a storage rack.

Moving on

Only two out of five new businesses survive the first three years The three failures are often caused by using too much working capital too quickly or paying salaries beyond the capacity of the business. I made no apology for arguing for a prudent development plan, slower than some wanted, and it was six years before we reached a comfortable turnover of £500,000. For years I had had in mind to retire from full-time work early enough to pursue other interests while I still had the energy. So, reaching sixty in 1987, I stood down as manager and members appointed Andrew Hibbert in my place.

We had agreed earlier that membership should be restricted to people working thirty hours or more, because part-timers had other priorities and Daily Bread asked for commitment. So I ceased to be a member and considered my work was done; Daily Bread was safely in orbit and perhaps needed a different style of manager to consolidate the business. I had noticed that co-operative entrepreneurs are sometimes reluctant to let go of the businesses they have influenced and this leads to much unhappiness. I continued to work part-time on packing herbs and spices for some years but took no further part in the decision-making process.

Visitors to Northampton frequently asked us to start another branch in Oxford, or Truro or Aberdeen, and we always said no because the business depended on the close-knit working group and co-operatives should not have subsidiaries. We encouraged enquirers to start similar wholefood co-operatives in their own locality and we offered loans, and advice about suppliers and staff exchanges as our contribution to co-operatives helping each other. We were also protective of the name, Daily Bread, but members made an exception when Andrew Hibbert was planning to move to Cambridge and wanted to set up a similar business. Daily Bread Co-operative (Cambridge) started in 1993 and is an independent co-operative business but linked with Northampton for joint bulk buying and mutual help.

Looking back at the seven years 1980-87, during which I was manager of Daily Bread Co-operative, I realise that they were the most creative years of my life. In retrospect, it also occurred to me that for several years I probably spent more time in prayer than ever before, not because of any individual discipline but because we adopted the corporate discipline of morning prayers at The Neighbours Community and I would then walk to work and, at coffee break, be involved in daily prayers at Daily Bread.

Writing this in 2016, the working group is 25 people and sales are around £1.5 million. The story has been told in several publications.*

*   *A New Thing – The story of Daily Bread Co-operative 1975-1985* by Jamie Wallace (Daily Bread Co-operative 1986)

    25 Years already? - crumbs. An insiders view by John Kerr (Daily Bread Co-operative 2005)

What of the future?

Ever since the industrial revolution there has been a prevailing view that industry must be an area of conflict. First it was owners versus workers in the early 19th century and later, as companies grew in size and complexity, it was managers versus unions, with owners providing the capital, standing back and taking the profits. This has been the mainstream but there is an evolutionary theory that radical step changes happen on the fringes, not in the mainstream but in more isolated groups experiencing different conditions.

In the middle of the 19th century, co-operatives emerged on the fringe, led by the Rochdale Pioneers and the Christian Socialists, a viable alternative to the excesses of capital ownership. Then, a hundred years later, another fringe flowering of worker co-operatives occurred in the 1970's and 1980's, of which Daily Bread Co-operative was a part and ICOM was the co-ordinating body. Partly it was a reaction to the Thatcher government's deliberately combative attitude for 'defeating' the miners and relying on unregulated market forces to bring about prosperity for all. In the event these policies certainly brought prosperity for some but also led to an increasing gap between the 'haves' and the 'have nots'. History indicates that, if unchecked, this inequality gap leads to violent revolution. Co-operatives provide part of this necessary check. In 1970 there were just ten employee-owned co-operatives listed, sometimes called worker co-operatives, but by 1988 this had grown to over 1800, before Thatcherism made their diminishment inevitable. When Co-operativesUK published an annual summary in 2008*, the year of financial meltdown, the number was down to less than 400.

* Co-operativesUK. Co-operative Review 2008 and subsequent years.

The abject failure of the banks in 2008 together with the disgust caused by excessive greed in the City and by remote shareholders, is sparking another outbreak of co-operatives which looks to be more firmly rooted than heretofore and possibly here to stay as a viable alternative structure for work. The annual summaries published by Co-operativesUK have shown a steady increase in numbers since 2008 and there are now over 5000 businesses in UK registered as co-operative societies rather than incorporated companies, some owned by customers and some by employees. Each of these businesses has objectives beyond the necessity to be financially viable and consequently these co-operatives expect a different style of management, less adversarial, more democratic, concentric rather than hierarchical. Although still a fringe, there are signs that the co-operative movement may well be moving into the mainstream and this will be a major evolutionary change during the present century.

Inevitably, due to the mass media, large organisations get the headlines and the John Lewis Partnership is the only employee-owned business widely known as a success and Triumph motorbikes the only widely known failure. The John Lewis constitution is too complex for it to be a blueprint and Triumph an unhappily named lesson to be learned, that busted conventional businesses cannot be magically turned into successful co-operatives. The growth will come from small businesses where all the members can sit round a table and communications are straightforward. There are plenty of well-established small employee-owned co-operatives like Daily Bread and this size constraint is unlikely to be an obstacle for growth as there are 700,000 businesses of twenty people or fewer in UK. Co-operativesUK offer straightforward constitutions, Model Rules, for establishing new businesses and continuing advances in electronic technology now enable much work to be done in small groups which previously required large numbers.

A further indication that co-operation is here to stay comes from the increasing number of women at work and their consequent influence on the way it is organised and led. Although there are plenty of examples of effective co-operative men, it has to be said that women are more natural co-operators. They are accustomed to multi-tasking and working in small non-hierarchical groups whereas men often want to dominate the group.

Although unregulated capitalism will not disappear in a hurry and some of its unregulated adherents will fight tooth and nail to preserve its inequalities, there are unmistakeable signs that this form of capitalism is dying,from the inside as well as the outside. The process is not dissimilar to the slow decline of communist ideology in USSR before the final break-up in December 1991. At the same time as capitalism is in moral decline, co-operative working, as an alternative to ownership solely by the suppliers of capital, is now moving from the fringe to the mainstream. Perhaps, as our grandchildren look back, the present time will be seen as the century of co-operation

Daily Bread Co-operative poster   2015

Rowan Williams, Archbishop of Canterbury 2002-2012,
at Daily Bread Co-operative to open the new on-line shop.
July 2013

S THE NEIGHBOURS COMMUNITY 1984-2007 (57-80)

Soon after we moved from Sheffield to Northampton in 1968 we were part of a house group of nine people, attached to St. Peter's Church of England parish church. We called it a 'cell group' and, later, a 'house communion group'. It became an influential part of our lives as we met every other Saturday for ten years, sharing a simple meal, studying the Bible, celebrating Holy Communion and discussing what it means to be Christians in the post-Christendom age.

From time to time the children got drawn into this group, whether they liked it or not, and we went away for a family holiday together every year at February half term, sometimes to Lee Abbey in Devon and sometimes to the Lake District. Often the discussion would revolve round the problems of being the church, the followers of Jesus, in the hedonistic surroundings of the 1970's.

In June 1974 I wrote an 'aunt sally' piece about the possibilities of community living. It refers to Acts 4:32 and suggests that 'existing terrace houses could be adapted'. We were not thinking of a 'commune' in which everyone lived together but a 'community of households' in which several families might live in separate houses, adjacent to each other, meeting daily for prayers as a 'house church', sharing some possessions and adopting some common social concerns. In the meantime, living in separate houses a mile apart, each cell family made a list of what might be shared. It became known as the 'lawnmower list' but also included three bicycles, a dog, a motor caravan, a sewing machine, a folk guitar and two spare beds.

By 1982, eight years after the aunt sally, I was working at Daily Bread Co-operative (see section R) and talking and writing about the possibilities of a more committed and sharing lifestyle. Susan was working as an Occupational Therapist at St Edmund's Hospital, our children were all away or at uni, and we were ready to make a move.

In the 1980's the concept of 'house church' was unusual and regarded with some apprehension by denominational bodies. Though less strident than Luther and without his theological training, we grumbled that some local congregations seemed to be dominated by priests and regarded the laity as 'pew-fodder'. We had the backing of our own parish priest who was a member of the house communion group and had the courage to keep a positive foot in both camps. There was a continuing debate about how we should carry forward the concept of a residential community and in due course this led to a search for a large house where we could all live under one roof. We looked at a building in Pitsford, just outside Northampton, and Grant Welch devised a blueprint for a purpose-built community house 'somewhere in the country'. This debate had far-reaching consequences and led to the disbanding of the house communion group in its original form. Grant and Rosemary moved to another parish in Norfolk, John Harper was appointed vicar of Caistor near Peterborough and Maurice Walton was accepted for training for ordination. The remaining four, Michael, Anne, Susan and myself, decided in 1982 to search for some adjoining terrace houses in Northampton where we could develop a Christian residential community.

Susan and I knew that a decision to move from our typical middle-class house in Weston Favell to an alternative uncertain lifestyle would turn our lives upside down and we made the decision with our eyes wide open. There were few precedents for the kind of community we had been discussing for years and we realised there would be all manner of problems to overcome. We reckoned it was 'only worth doing' if we regarded it as a twenty year project. In the event ,we stayed for over 23 years.

In 1968, I had got to know Michael Jones because he was planning to turn the family jeweller's business, which he had inherited, to employee-ownership.* I was able to assist with preparing the constitution to transform the business into a registered co-operative society under the Industrial&Provident Societies Acts (IPSA).

* Michael published his story, *It May Be Christian. I Think it's Silly,*
  in 2009. ISBN 978-0-9562217-0-4 At the time of writing (2016),
  Michael Jones Jeweller continues to flourish as an employee-owned
  business with more than 30 people at work and sales of over £5 million.

Anne Jones had initially worked at the local newspaper and considered a career as a journalist but later qualified as a teacher with a degree in English Literature.   Michael was a Reader in the Church of England and both of them had been members of the house communion group since its inception.

We realised that finding three adjoining houses for sale at the same time was a very long shot. One day we looked at a house in Ardington Road, in a suburban area of Northampton, which seemed right. It was solidly built and had a long back garden facing south. But we needed three houses, not just one.   So Michael knocked at the door of the adjacent house and said, "Excuse me for asking but I wonder if your house is for sale?". The young man who answered door said, "Strange you should ask because my mother died recently and I am about to put this house on the market. Come in and look round". I knocked on the door on the other side and was confronted by a friendly grey-haired woman.   "Excuse me for asking but I wonder if your house is for sale?". She replied, "Strange you should ask because my sister lives across the road and we have just agreed to share her house. So this one will be for sale, come in and have a look". This seemed like an answer to our prayers and within a few weeks we had bought all three houses.

A member of the house communion group, Maurice Walton, was a distinguished architect and drew up an imaginative plan to turn the three houses into a flexible community house with communicating doors and ten bedrooms. From the road the houses were unchanged but once inside the door it was quite different. The 'front room' of the middle house became our meeting room and, as a symbolic act of sharing property, we knocked down the middle two fences to make a large back garden. Michael and Anne moved into 146 in June 1983, while the builders reconstructed 142 and 144. They were covered in dust for six months but were then able to move into 142 while the builders renovated 146. After a further six months the alterations were completed, enabling Susan and I move in.

So The Neighbours Community was born on 29 June 1984 and, in due course, incorporated daily morning worship in the community room set aside for the purpose, occasions such as communion services, agape suppers (see Appendix VI Sharing Bread and Wine, and Appendix VII An Agape Liturgy) prayers in the style of Taizé, prayer groups for healing, and shared bible study groups. Later we added two further adjacent houses to make five in all.

During the early years we had many discussions about the purpose of the project and members had differing ideas about what we were trying to do but it was not until 1997 that we adopted a concise statement :-

The purpose of The Neighbours is to develop a Christian community life which enables us to share and explore our faith and care for others, according to the Gospel.

This statement was printed on all our programmes thereafter and remained unchanged until the project ended in 2007. I noted a quotation from Dietrich Bonhoeffer, the Protestant pastor who opposed Hitler and was executed by the Gestapo in 1944:-

> ' The renewal of the church will come from a new type of monasticism which may only have in common with the old an uncompromising allegiance to the Sermon on the Mount. It is high time men and women banded together to do this. '

> 'The Life and Death of Dietrich Bonhoeffer'. Mary Bosanquet
> (Hodder & Stoughton 1958) p.150

For better or for worse we *banded together* between 1984 and 2007. Susan and I were the only people to be part of The Neighbours Community for the whole of its life and a total of over fifty people lived in the Community houses at one time or another. This figure does not include friends or relatives coming for a visit but does include people who needed some support, usually on discharge from psychiatric hospital. They were invited by the members to rent room space and join in the life of the Community, including meals, prayers and social events. Some stayed a few weeks and some for several years. Some took an active part in the corporate life, others almost no part.

During the last quarter of the 20th. Century there was a proliferation of small lay Christian residential communities.

From 1993 to 1997 I was editor of *Christian Community*, the magazine of the National Association of Christian Communities and Networks (NACCAN) and the Directory, published in 2000 listed 135 such groups – little known but significant outposts of the post-Christendom church.

The full story of The Neighbours Community is told in my book *Under One Roof*, published by Darton Longman & Todd in 2015 (ISBN 978-0-232-53173-2), with a Foreword by Jean Vanier, founder of the L'Arche communities.

T FAITH JOURNEY 1927 to present date

My earliest recollection of any kind of concern about a spiritual path was listening to my mother reading Bible stories to us. As children we used to have a rest after lunch (I still do at 89), lying on the floor while she read to us and worked at her knitting at the same time. Every few minutes she had to pause to check the stitches so we experienced a silence which could be contemplative. Before long we would say "*go on, mum, get on with the story even if you have a dropped stitch in those socks*". Both she and my father were people of firm Christian faith although neither of them found it easy to talk about their beliefs. When she died I discovered from her Bible that my mother read it through, year by year, from cover to cover, noting the dates in the margin. She was a gentle person and a wonderful example for which I remain constantly grateful. My father expressed his faith mainly by being a churchwarden, money raiser, administrator, rather than verbally. As a teenager, when I asked him what he believed he said the Apostles Creed in the Book of Common Prayer was all he needed and left it at that.

Christian faith and Sunday churchgoing were taken for granted in our household . At Arnold House, the school in North Wales where David and I were boarders for much of the 1930's, two sons of the Bishop of Chester were fellow pupils and therefore Geoffrey Fisher, who later became Archbishop of Canterbury, was an occasional visitor. We slept in dormitories of about 12 boys and Bishop Fisher told us it would be an example of moral courage for a boy to kneel beside his bed and say his prayers before going to sleep. Mudford, aged about 13, feared no foe and claimed to be an agnostic or even, shock/horror, an atheist, said " *Wouldn't it be an even better example of moral courage, sir, if there was a dormitory of bishops and one of them **did not** kneel beside his bed ?* ". I don't recollect the episcopal response to this challenge.

I was routinely confirmed into membership of the Church of England as a teenager at Bedford School but it made little impression on me, but later, an experience as a young student had a profound effect on my spiritual journey. A barnstorming American evangelist, appropriately named Doctor Barnhouse, conducted a mission at Great St.Mary's, Cambridge in 1946 and caused me to have the only 'religious experience' of my life so far. For the first time I became aware and convinced that the Jesus of the Gospels was indeed fully God as well as fully man, that God/Jesus loved me and wished to enter into some kind of communication with me and this would change the orientation of my life. Somehow, all the preaching and teaching at school and all the tedious Matins I sat through at our local parish church at home had never before convinced me of these basic Christian beliefs. This conviction stays with me to this day.

When I went to work in Rugby in 1948, my response to the Cambridge experience was to join an evangelical Church of England congregation. The children of the enthusiastic church members joined the Scout or Guide troops but there was also a residue of less enthusiastic boys who became the Crusader class and I was one of their Sunday School teachers with flannel board and somewhat hesitant exhortation. They were unresponsive and one boy routinely escaped and hid in the outside loo; we had to pour buckets of cold water over the door as the only way to get him out. The strange thing was that these boys continued to come to the class rather than play hookey but I never knew how many converts we made.

Within a year or two my evangelical fervour was waning and I began to question some of the fundamentalist teaching. Unquestioning acceptance of some of the dodgier Bible passages seemed too simplistic and, at least for me, failed to get to the heart of the Gospels.   My faith was undimmed but I searched for more depth.   For example, there is historical evidence of a Great Flood but the Genesis story, chapters 6-7, was surely mythical rather than numerically accurate. This did not mean that the story was untrue but the spiritual meaning of it mattered more than the precise number of zebras that walked up the gangplank onto the ark. 'Noah' is all of us and the Genesis writer was describing a profound experience rather than recording facts. So argued the young engineering graduate, who spent a considerable time at work recording facts and figures and enjoying it.

Moreover, I was not impressed with some of the church elders who were also senior managers at one or other of the Rugby large engineering works. They were enthusiastic about saving souls but seemed uninterested in debating Christian principles at work, and I wanted to be a Monday Christian rather than only a Sunday one. So when I left Rugby to work in Sheffield I went to the nearest parish church rather than seek out a specifically evangelical congregation and over the years I have moved further away from church hierarchies.   I am truly grateful for the preaching which led me to accept that Jesus is fully divine as well as fully human and, of course, there is a Gospel imperative to preach the good news but such preaching is not my gift.   Susan claims that I am still a covert evangelical but, if so, it is very covert.

At work, swiftly ascending the management ladder, I worried about the injustices I saw in the relations between owners, managers and workers. My quest continued, not only for some guidance regarding personal behaviour at work but also for structures which could better reflect the Gospel priorities than the incorporated Companies Acts model. In these Acts, the existence of employees is not mentioned and the purpose of the business is confined to optimising the interests of the shareholders who are the owners. It seemed to me that we needed to engage more with 'the principalities and powers' that Paul was concerned about in Ephesians 6:12 .

The Spear & Jackson tradition was that Directors should also be shareholders so when the Board invited me to be a Director in 1957, I was expected to buy some shares to qualify. I hesitated, but our Chairman, Jack Haggie, who had no scruples about the ownership of the company, thinking that I did not have the money, presented me with 700 shares which he had bought in my name. He did not quite say, 'enough of this nonsense', but I realised that he was keen to 'get me on board' by means of this generous gesture. So I weakened, and paid him for them. As a shareholder, albeit a reluctant one, and a Director, I had begun to realise that I was part of the problem rather than part of the answer. So when I left, some ten years later, I sold them and have never owned any equity shares since.

Coming across the Sheffield Industrial Mission was a breath of fresh air. Led by Ted Wickham, the industrial chaplains were largely independent of the local church congregations and Ted claimed that working men had not been sitting in church pews for over a hundred years. *

*Church & People in an Industrial City, by E.R.Wickham, (Lutterworth Press 1957)

The industrial chaplains in Sheffield were listening to men and women in their work environment, concerned with the ethical problems of their work but having no church background and no other framework of reference. Jesus' great commandment was about love of God and love of neighbour, and prophet Micah had thundered, 700 years before Jesus, that what our God required of us was that we should *'do justly, love tenderly and walk humbly'*.

Where was the justice on the shop floor? Where was the love/agape between colleagues and where was the humility of those in positions of influence, be they shareholders, managers or trade unionists. A picture of Ted Wickham talking with a group round a coke brazier in a steelworks melting shop, shows the Industrial Mission's response to some of these questions. The faces of his audience express thoughtfulness, even excitement rather than indifference as Ted talked about justice and equality and love as the message of the Gospels. And there too was Leslie Hunter, Bishop of Sheffield, sitting amongst the steelworkers.

Recollecting Ted's challenge that Susan and I must become 'catalysts', I threw myself into this groud-breaking mission activity, encouraged Margaret Kane, the chaplain attached to our works, sat in on some of her workplace meetings and became secretary of an out-of-hours manager's group, meeting at our house. Michael Adie, vicar of the parish church where we lived in Broomhill, became a good friend and said he did not expect to see me much in church because my priority should be the 'wider church' in industry. Our daughter Mary was baptised at the monthly Industrial Mission communion service in the crypt of Sheffield Cathedral. We were an 'industrial mission family'.

Ted also became a valued friend of ours and when he was appointed Bishop of Middleton we went to his Consecration at York Minster in a special train full of the many steel workers with whom he had been working for years.   The Dean and Chapter processed slowly up the nave, slowly because the speed of a convoy is the speed of the slowest ship and some of these clergy 'ships' were surprisingly old and infirm. From the pew behind us I heard a loud whisper: *"Twer'e best they put 'em all on a trolley and dragged 'em up the church".* The speaker had probably never been to such a service before but steelworkers knew how to move heavy loads.*

* In 2015 we were at York Minster again for the Consecration of Alison White, only the second woman to become a bishop in UK. Apart from episcopal friends, in the intervening half century, we did not have much formal contact with bishops, except for the wonderful occasion in 2013 when Rowan Williams, former Archbishop of Canterbury, came to Daily Bread Co-operative to inaugurate the on-line shop.

Another Industrial Mission incident which has influenced my faith journey ever since was our discovery of Taizé, an interdenominational monastic community in the middle of France. In 1968 Leslie Hunter, Bishop of Sheffield, invited some of the Taizé Brothers to visit Whirlow Grange, the diocesan conference centre. Taking Ruth with us in her carry-cot, we spent an evening with them, sitting in a circle on the floor of the chapel singing their chants, interspersed with periods of silent reflection, not unlike a Quaker meeting. The repetitive singing of these chants was a new experience for us and now they have become known all over the world. The recollection of this occasion has remained with me for over half a century and worship in the style of Taizé has been part of our life during all of this time.

One of the brothers, Frère Thomas, stayed in Sheffield for some months and worked as a labourer in the steel melting department at Spear&Jackson. He had little English but picked up some useful Yorkshire phrases from his fellow-workers. Also Frère Jan, an experienced children's psychologist from The Netherlands, stayed in Sheffield for a year during which we came to know him well and kept in touch until he died twenty years later. He found work as a porter at Sheffield Children's Hospital where Susan had also worked, as an occupational therapist, before our marriage. This was the Taizé pattern of ministry the Brothers adopted wherever they were in the world, to work for their living at the very bottom of the employment ladder and be a quiet Christian presence of service. Some years later we visited Taizé in our motor caravan and Frère Jan, with a strong continental accent, read Winnie the Pooh to the children in their bunks at bedtime. Thereafter we returned there numerous times, and have been strongly influenced by their concern for Christian unity, their worship, simple lifestyle and identification with the poorest people around them. For me the latter were people oppressed by work in industry, or the mentally ill or, later, refugees from violence in the Middle East.

After leaving Spear & Jackson in 1966 I spent a term back in Cambridge and my neighbour across the landing was Maurice Wiles, an authority on the early fathers of the church. He kindly offered to guide my reading and spend an hour each week discussing it. A generous offer by a leading scholar and busy professorial teacher (see also section K). I did some reading around the concept of the Kingdom of God, concluding that the best evidence was that the Kingdom was present in the here and now, whenever God's will was being done, but also we were to look forward to a greater realisation of the Kingdom at some unknown future time, the second coming of Christ. The Kingdom was here and still to come. When we moved to Northampton in 1968 with the task of developing

Trylon as an employee-owned co-operative business, Susan had little opportunity to make new contacts because of the demands of four children. I was busy, working all hours, and not giving as much attention to the family as I should. My view was that Trylon, a very small radical experiment in ownership and democratic management, was more likely to succeed if the working group were fellow Christians with a Gospel-based agenda.   After much debate, the Trylon group of working members eventually agreed in 1973 on a Preamble which stated that the business was :-

> 'a practical attempt to create an industrial society
> based on Christian principles ....We wish to build
> a self-governing community .... expressing through
> our work our shared belief in the spiritual nature of
> man.'

Big words for a tiny business. We paid some attention to this concern through prayer and occasional events such as a carol service at Christmas.

Apart from work, the main event in my faith journey as we settled into Northampton was the formation of the house communion group, based on St.Peter's Parish Church in Weston Favell, where we lived. This group, described in Section S, developed a pattern of a simple supper together, incorporating a eucharistic liturgy and then a talk by one of the group and discussion. This group met for ten years and because of this continuity, we got to know each other well and it was a safe place to share our hopes and fears, convictions and doubts. For me it was the best 'church' I had yet encountered and although we continued to attend the parish church, the house group was my primary place of worship.   My search for integration of work and worship, for a business with social objectives, was a frequent topic of discussion by the group and the nine house group members became the initial Members of Daily Bread Co-operative in 1975.

Together with others, I wrote a liturgy, *A Simple Communion - arranged for house meetings and small gatherings,* and formed a vestigial publishing house, Disciples Press, to give it some circulation. With the ongoing experience of the group I also wrote a booklet *The Church That Meets in Your House* which was published by Daily Bread Co-operative in 1980. We claimed, with plenty of back up from the Gospel writers, that Jesus' concept of the church was inevitably made up of small groups meeting in each other's houses to share food and worship, long before the first church buildings appeared. The American anthropologist, Margaret Mead (1901-1978) wrote:-

> *'Never doubt that a small group of thoughtful committed citizens can change the world - indeed, it is the only thing that ever has.'*

Desmond Tutu said, "*When I pray co-incidences happen*". One of the 'co-incidences' that happened to us was the gradual emergence of Daily Bread as a viable employee-owned business. Another co-incidence, at the beginning of The Neighbours Community was the statistical improbability of finding three adjacent houses, 142,144,146 Ardington Road, then adding 148 due to Dorothy Seamark's friendship, followed by Rosalind Bellerby's loan to buy 140 in 1986 Surely the Holy Spirit was working in this place during those busy years.

Redundant church buildings abound in Northampton and throughout UK. Some continue as significant historic buildings but others have been changed into dwelling houses or office premises. It seems this trend will continue and my faith journey has led me to the view that the pattern of the church, the body of Christian believers, in this century is likely to be towards house churches and agape worship.   The great Cathedrals will surely remain as places for large gatherings of the faithful but the week-to-week worship is likely to be in small house groups as it was in the early church, described in the Gospels, the Acts of the Apostles and Paul's letters. All three Gospel references to the bread and wine ceremony are within the context of a meal (Mathew 26:26-30, Mark 14:22-25, Luke 22:14-20.) These thoughts are set out in more depth in Appendix VI, *Sharing Bread and Wine: reclaiming the concept of agape.*

When The Neighbours came to a natural end in 2007, Susan and I moved into a flat at Old School House at the end of the same road, where we have maintained the daily morning prayer discipline, taking it in turns to lead a simple liturgy of Bible reading and intercessory prayers. Susan has been an active member of the local Quaker meeting for over twenty years and I have developed a roving pattern of churchgoing, attending sometimes the nearby parish church, sometimes going to Sunday Mass at Turvey Abbey, a Benedictine community near Bedford, sometimes to the local United Reformed Church and sometimes going to the Quaker meeting with Susan.   The negative consequence is that I am not an active member of any congregation but the corresponding positive result is that I am an interdenominational person and make some kind of contribution to unity, for we are indeed all members of the wider Christian church.   I note that, as well as my parents (staunch C. of E.), and my wife (staunch Quaker), the people who have had most influence on my journey are from four different Christian denominations :   Charlie Moule and Ted Wickham (Church of England), Jack Bellerby (Methodist),

George Macleod (Church of Scotland), Fritz Schumacher (Roman Catholic).

So, in conclusion, this has been my faith journey. Many pray for faith and I believe it is a charism, a gift of God, seemingly given to some but not to all, so I am continuously thankful for this gift which has given meaning and purpose to my life. During the 70 years since that experience at Cambridge my faith has wavered from time to time, bruised but never shattered, dented but not destroyed.

I have always believed that there is life beyond death and it makes sense to me that our life on earth is some kind of preparation for a fuller life after death. I have held on to the concept of the Kingdom, simultaneously present with us now and also expected in its fullness in the future . I have not been too bothered about the form of such afterlife. Will we be united with those we have loved ?   Will we be aware of what is happening on earth? My concerns, for better or for worse, have been more about the search for a Gospel-centred lifestyle here and now.

> *'Seek ye first the kingdom of God... and all these things*
> *shall be added unto you .'*   *(Matthew 6:33 AV)*
> or
> *'Strive first for the kingdom of God and ... and all these*
> *things will be given to you as well.' (NRSV)*

U EDUCATION SERVICES 1976-2016

Jack and Rosalind Bellerby were a wonderful couple of Oxford academics. Jack had been appointed Professor of Economics at Liverpool University in 1930 but stood down a few years later. He was aware of the inequalities of UK society in the 1930's and, in a typical but very unusual move, he decided to put his principles into practice by living on the average wage of the day, three pounds per week, and giving away the balance of his professorial salary. He also stood for Parliament as a candidate for the Labour Party.

At Cambridge he was part of a discussion group with J.M. Keynes and wrote extensively on economics and agriculture, setting out his philosophy in *A Contributive Society* * in 1931, including support for co-operatives. This brought us together in the 1970's when I was self-employed and we had many discussions about how to put some of his ideas into practice. For example, he considered that if enough people are willing to pay a little above the market price for food and this extra is returned to the producer in the developing world, then there would be a significant improvement in the quality of life. The term Fairtrade was unknown in his lifetime but has blossomed and expanded hugely during the first decade of the 21st. century. Jack would be delighted.

* *A Contributive Society* (Education Services 1931), re-printed with additional papers in 1988

A more fundamental example is the need to re-distribute income and wealth. A reviewer of *A Contributive Society* wrote:-

> '*It may be regarded as a companion volume to*
> *Mr. Tawney's 'Acquisitive Society', for while*
> *Mr Tawney is mainly occupied with the*
> *fundamental disease of our economic system,*
> *Mr. Bellerby tries to point the way to a new order.*'

Jack was a 'doer' as well as a thinker and his ideas were fundamentally influenced by his abiding Christian faith. When Education Services reprinted the book in 1988, Sir Austin Robinson, Professor Emeritus of Economics at Cambridge, wrote in his Foreword :-

> '*The thinking of the book is the complete antithesis*
> *of much currently dominant economic doctrine and*
> *the argument that the more selfish we are, the*
> *more we shall benefit the human race. It (the book)*
> *is built on the idea that one should concern oneself*
> *with the treatment of one's neighbours. That*
> *philosophy is by no means dead. Bellerby will be*
> *remembered .... for this book and its consequences.*'

Austin Robinson also wrote, '*in some curious way the institutions that Bellerby inspired have survived.*'

Jack termed his philosophy 'contributive'. His concept of a 'contributive person' was one who put more into society than he or she took out and his thesis was that if there was a sufficient number of such people, there would be a net improvement in the quality of life for everyone. Input might be in terms of time, ideas, or money. He wanted to bring together groups of contributive people, and initiated a charitable fund, Education Services, to make grants to them. As an academic, he envisaged that such grants would be primarily around education, hence the name.

The two most significant counter-cultural projects of my life story,Daily Bread Co-operative and The Neighbours Community, both owe some of their contributive philosophy to Jack who spent years, like me, seeking for practical ways to express his deeply-held Christian faith. He was wounded in World War I and lost an arm but that did not deter him from writing prolifically about agricultural economics. Rosalind, his wife and lifelong companion, became his amanuensis and, in a sense, I became the son they never had. He insisted on paying for some of my writing about employee-ownership to be published in the 1980's.

Jack worked at the Agricultural Economics Unit at Oxford during the latter part of his career and was a familiar figure, cycling in crowded streets despite the inconvenience of having only one arm.   He could also tie his own shoelaces and successfully challenged others in time trials !

Jack died in 1977 aged 80, and therefore he never saw Daily Bread Co-operative which Rosalind declared was the best outworking of his philosophy. She spent years collecting and editing his papers and donated a beautiful tapestry which hangs in the meeting room at Daily Bread.

They were both inspirational people in my life. After 40 years as a member of Education Services, I stood down in 2016 but Ruth has also been a member for years and so maintains the family connection.

V NATIONAL FRIENDSHIP FUND
- 'on the back of an envelope'　　1975-2016

'Unprecedented in history, masses of humanity do not live, nor will they be buried, where they were born. The great migration of the dead. War did this first, and then water.'

Anne Michaels *The Winter Vault*

'War did this first'. Caradog Jones was a Quaker and university lecturer who was sentenced to three months hard labour in Newcastle Gaol, as a pacifist and conscientious objector in the first world war. He spent three years in solitary confinement, sewing mailbags. On release he had to rebuild his career as an academic statistician but he also became a dedicated peace worker and founded the National Friendship Fund (NFF) in 1956, to help refugees displaced by the second world war. He wrote :-

> *' it would be surprising if friends would ever want to fight each other. A step in the right direction, therefore, would be to foster friendly relations – in place of fear and enmity - between different nations..... Individuals can take the initiative and do in a small way what governments do in a big way …. so together we shall be doing something to promote peace throughout the world.'*

Caradog assumed in his writing at the time that the number of refugees would gradually diminish but, in fact, half a century later, there are more refugees worldwide. For example, in the UK there are Afghanis, Syrians, Eritreans and Congolese, all of whom are refugees due to international or civil wars. The future looks little different and it seems that ' war refugees ' will be a continuing feature of western European society and will continue to be a controversial subject.

Caradog was said to have run the NFF 'on the back of an envelope'. When he died, in 1974, his friend Ben Bennett became the administrative trustee and Ben handed the work on to me in 1981. For over fifty years it has remained a small registered charity and has had a special concern for Eritrea since 1990 when the Fund received a generous grant from a Quaker who had travelled there.   Refugees from Eritrea, managing to escape from a vicious military dictatorship, often without money or identification papers, have stories of extraordinary perseverance and suffering in making their way to the UK. In 2009, one young Eritrean travelled through the channel tunnel under a Eurostar train and almost died of exposure.

Anne Michaels' novel is not about war but describes the displacement of twenty thousand Nubians during the building of the Aswan Dam in the 1960's. Lake Nasser now stretches 300 kilometres along the Nile. She then moves the story to Canada where large numbers of Canadians were 're-located' to make room for the St. Lawrence Seaway.

In addition to wars and construction, it is likely that we shall soon see 'water refugees' - people fleeing from regions where increased population is causing conflict for limited water supplies. Palestine and Israel both depend on the Jordan river; Ethiopia, Eritrea, Sudan and Egypt argue about the distribution of water from the Nile and the damming of Amazon tributaries is already causing problems.   Anne Michaels' words are coming true. Travelling to the remote northern area of Eritrea in 2000, for the National Friendship Fund, James Linell and I stopped for a coffee break at Afabet. There by chance, or was it providence, we happened to meet Sister Thomas, university lecturer, missionary sister for 40 years in Eritrea. We saw the shipping container in which she had lived when she first came to this village; it had *Scotland For Ever* painted on the side. When we told her we were concerned about drinking water she took us to see a well into which a donkey had fallen, dragging with it the young boy who was leading it. Both were drowned and the well was contaminated and unusable, a triple tragedy for a village that desperately needed clean drinking water. We had brought a donation to NFF from Ann Hobbis, a friend in Northampton, so we changed our dollars into Nakfa and gave her a wad of notes more than an inch thick.

Two years later we were in Afabet again. After long delays due to the border war with Ethiopia which was causing a shortage of manpower and building materials, the resourceful Sister Thomas had arranged for a local contractor, "*an honest man*", to reconstruct the well. His team had emptied it and dug down a further two metres to make a total depth of nine metres, adding considerably to the amount of water available. They had lined it with stone and cemented the joints. There were people coming and going with buckets and a small oasis of fruit trees was growing round the well. They intend to put a cover over it and build a wall to prevent small children and stray animals from falling into it. This well will be of great benefit to the many people living on this site. The money may run to adding a hand-operated pump but, if not, a rope and plastic jerrycans will suffice. Although many Eriteans are active Muslims or Christians, the state is strictly secular and Sister Thomas said, " *We are not here to convert but to do the will of God in this place, to feed the hungry, and relieve the oppressed. That's why we need this well.*" We returned to the missionary compound and in the sister's little chapel we prayed something like:-

'Thank you, Lord, for peace in this land which has enabled us, at last, to rebuild this well, so much needed by your people, both Christian and Muslim. May the water not only refresh our bodies but also be a refreshment to our spirits and renew our concern to do your will in this place. We give thanks for Ann whose generosity has made this rebuilding possible, demolishing the barriers of geography and culture and showing us that we are indeed one Church and that we acknowledge one Lord. Alleluia.'

From Afabet we travelled further north to a new school at Nakfa and then returned to Keren where Johannes and his daughter, Nasret, took us to see another well being dug near their home village of Musha.   Johannes is a local building contractor and water expert. He is 90 years old and tells us that the one thing he wants to do before he dies is to provide a well in this village where he was born.   A man of serious purpose, highly respected in the local community.

There is no road to Musha and although a four-wheel drive can just about get there over the stony terrain, it seems more appropriate to walk the last kilometre, a pilgrim walk for us, joining with children, donkeys and camels coming from the existing more distant well.   This is a two hour round journey for them and it has to be made twice a day to bring sufficient water to the village, so no wonder they hope for success for the new well which is much nearer.

Six young men are digging the well with pick and shovel, breaking up the shale rock with a hammer and cold chisel, working in two gangs of three, turn and turn about. It is three metres in diameter and they are ten metres down, advancing at about half a metre a week. Back breaking work. They have not found water yet and some locals say that the water table has dropped so much that they will not get to it.   Johannes disagrees. He encourages his cheerful digging team, Habte, Drar, Yosuf and Essayas, shouting down to them, "*Courage ! Coraggio ! We are on the brink of victory.*" There is a sense of urgency as the well shaft must be lined and sealed before the 'big rains' come in June, otherwise the topsoil will be washed into the well shaft and it will be unusable. For me, it is hard work just climbing up the makeshift ladder from ten metres down, let alone using a pick or shovel, but Johannes in Churchillian tones says, *"We shall dig to 15 metres or even 20 metres. We shall never give up."*

Arriving in the village we are invited to the coffee ceremony at the house of the village elder, Weldu, who is 84 and apologises for being in his work clothes instead of the spotless white robe in which he would normally greet visitors. Perhaps we are the only Europeans he has entertained since our last visit in 2000. Formal greeting are exchanged in a tangled mixture of English, Italian and Tigrinya, the local language.

Musha is a Christian village and they show us their 'church house', a round tukul with a straw roof just like all the other houses but with no furniture except a simple altar. We stand on the mud floor and say a silent prayer, giving thanks for the faith of these remarkable people and praying that they will strike water at the well.   He asks for nothing more but I realise that he will need more to dig to the greater depth and buy the cement for the lining. So I give him 13,000 Nakfa from the National Friendship Fund and he is grateful and says this will be sufficient to pay the digging team for a further ten weeks, and for the cement. He shows me the meticulous accounts he has kept for the NFF donation. Searching for a quotation I think of Luke 10:35 and say something like, *"Take care of the well and when I come back this way, we will pay you whatever else you spend on it."* We say goodbye to this wonderful man and I notice there are tears in his eyes, as there are in mine. A man of integrity, dignity and faith, *"... we are on the brink of victory."*

This story does not yet have a happy ending. Visiting again two years later, in 2004, we learned that the drought in this part of Eritrea is such that the well did not fill, even at 18 metres down. I was saddened when they showed us the puddle of water at the bottom, hardly enough to fill a bucket, but they are used to deprivation and hardship and were amazingly cheerful and resilient. *"We will dig further to 20 metres"*, they said, the maximum practicable depth for hand digging, but if there is still no water the whole village may have to be moved to another location to be nearer a water supply.

During the 35 years I have been the administrator of the NFF the policy of the Trustees has been to make grants with whatever money is donated and not to build reserves. Small is beautiful. During this time the Fund has made over 1000 grants, mostly to young Eritrean refugees in UK but also to schools and agricultural projects in Eritrea. Now in my 90th. year I am happy to hand on the Fund to others because there is still work to do to realise Caradog Jones' vision of friendship between people of different

W   OLD SCHOOL HOUSE   (2007 to present date)

We had looked at Old School House twenty years previously, when it was nearly derelict and for sale (see *Under One Roof* page 31) and had decided then that it was far larger than we needed for The Neighbours supportive housing project. It was bought by Anglia Building Society who restructured the old house into six flats and built thirty more in what had been the headmaster's spacious garden.   In November 2006 Susan and I had given the agreed twelve months notice to leave The Neighbours and in June 2007, soon after my eightieth birthday, we signed up to buy Flat 20 which faces south and is one of four flats which form the connecting passage between the old and the new buildings.

> With the help of our car and a wheelbarrow making about a hundred journeys we moved gradually over several months without the need of a removal van. This manual operation enabled us to make a smooth transfer and put stuff where we wanted it but, in retrospect, it took a lot of energy and we needed at least six months to recover. We do not recommend it.

At Old School House the resident-owners must be '*over 55 years of age and capable of living independently*'. The usual pattern in Northampton for blocks of flats is that the developer sells the flats but retains the freehold and ownership of the communal areas. This enables him not only to make a capital profit on the building work but also to receive a continuing revenue from the service charge for managing the block. However, in the case of Old School House one of the early flat owners in 1988, Bob Bossom OBE, was an experienced housing administrator and he recommended that the flat owners form themselves into a limited company, Old School House (Northampton) Ltd., which purchased the leasehold from the developer. Thus each flat owner becomes a voting member of the company and the block is independent of the developer and is wholly owned by the residents. In other words it is a co-operative or self-governing community, so we moved from one pattern of community living to another. The average age of resident owners is just over eighty and we appoint the directors each year at the AGM. Susan, being just under the average, agreed to be a director for the first year or two and I followed her in 2010 and served for four years. At our age, directors sometimes cannot easily remember what they have decided or not decided but, by and large, we manage quite well and it is a far more satisfactory arrangement than being in the hands of external managers who are being paid to make a profit for outside shareholders.

APPENDIX I   DAILY BREAD CO-OPERATIVE - PREAMBLE

Daily Bread Co-operative Ltd. was registered under the terms of the Industrial & Provident Societies Act (1965) on 2 March 1976, Registered Society No. 21612R, the first of many co-operative enterprises to use the new ICOM Model Rules. A founding document, Preamble, setting out the purposes of this registration, was signed by the nine Founder Members on 15 November 1975 :-

PREAMBLE (1975)

The early co-operative movement in the 19th century was concerned with social justice and spiritual values within a commercial framework. It included manufacturing enterprises, but in this century very few industrial co-operatives have been started and the Rules of the old ones are complex and unsuitable for to-day. The Industrial Common Ownership Movement (ICOM) have prepared a simple updated set of Model Rules for a registered co-operative society which will be a self-governing enterprise, owned and controlled by the people working in it.

One reason for starting the Daily Bread Co-operative is to demonstrate the procedure for forming this kind of enterprise and to make the Model Rules available at very low cost to others who may wish to follow. These enterprises will be deliberately and inextricably bound up with the industrial and commercial society in which we find ourselves. As its name implies Daily Bread is struggling with the problems of earning a living by making a product or providing a service.

In addition to this outward and visible reason, we are aware of other influences which have led us to take this initiative. As a cell group of committed Christians we have been celebrating the eucharist in each other's homes for two years, and discussing our beliefs and aspirations. We look for a lifestyle in which work and worship and recreation are all bound together. For work to be an enriching experience we believe there must be a concern for the body, mind and spirit; these needs cannot be isolated from each other. As five families incorporating twenty two people we hope to preserve the joy we experience in our separate family lives, but also we see the need to share with one another and to care for each other, and for people outside the group, at greater depth than we find possible when living in separate dispersed houses.

Therefore Daily Bread may provide the structure for integrating work and worship, a church without walls, or some kind of living community. It is an act of faith. We do not have a clear plan for what it may become, nor do we anticipate who may be involved in it.

John Harper	Roger Sawtell (secretary)	Maurice Walton
Anne Jones	Susan Sawtell	Grant Welch
Michael Jones	Gillian Walton	Rosemary Welch (chairman)

Founder Members. November 15th. 1975

It is clear from this *Preamble* that the group was thinking not only about starting a business but also about some kind of residential community. In the event Daily Bread Co-operative did not start trading until 1980, five years after the *Preamble* was signed. During those years, there was much discussion about the incipient business (and the living community which eventually came to birth as The Neighbours Community in 1984).

When the wholefood business was becoming established, a totally revised version of the *Preamble* was agreed in 1982, after a long process of discussion by the working members, including two of the Founding Members, Roger Sawtell and Anne Jones. This document, which has stood unaltered for over thirty years (2016), concentrated on setting out the five 'fundamentals'.

PREAMBLE (1982)

WORK is fundamental. We wish to earn our living by working together in a relationship which is enriching and creative and which values each individual. As a worker co-operative we will share the policy decisions which affect our work and share the financial results of it, in good times and in bad.

FOOD is fundamental. We wish to trade as suppliers of wholefoods which have good nutritional value and are good value for money.

OTHER PEOPLE are fundamental. We will have an ongoing concern for people recovering from mental disorders, by offering them employment in a supportive setting and by assisting them to return to open society.

THE WORLD is fundamental. We will not retreat from the world around us but will endeavour to develop an enterprise which is viable in the market economy in which we find ourselves. We recognise that we are part of the rich world rather than a part of the deprived world, but we do not accept that contemporary value judgements and trade patterns are unchangeable. Therefore we shall give a significant percentage of our total remuneration to causes outside the co-operative, with special reference to Third World causes.

COMMITMENT is fundamental. We are a fellowship. We will have a discipline of prayer and worship together. We will care for each other. Our inspiration comes from Jesus Christ. What we do is a venture of faith and we believe it will succeed just as far as we discern God's will and act upon it.

TOGETHER WE SET OUR HANDS TO THESE TASKS

Note:- The information in this appendix is taken from
'A NEW THING - the story of Daily Bread Co-operative 1975-1985', written by Jamie Wallace, with information researched by Adam York and drawings by Jane Walton, published in 1986. The title was inspired by a verse from the Old Testament, '*I am about to do a new thing; now it springs forth. Do you not perceive it ?*' (Isaiah 43:19 NRSV).

Jamie Wallace writes in the Introduction, 'To-day (1985) Daily Bread is well established commercially, with an annual turnover of £400,000 and some progress made toward the achievement of the *Preamble*'s less tangible objectives. Both commercial success and idealogical progress have come about through years of thought, discussion, prayer and physical effort on the part of many people. And the story is not over yet.'

Adam York moved on to become a founder member of Unicorn Grocery a similar wholefood worker co-operative in Manchester which opened in 1996 and now (2016) has over 60 working members and a turnover of £7 million.

EMPLOYEE-OWNED CO-OPERATIVE BUSINESSES IN THE 1970's
AND THEIR LEGACY FOR THE 21st CENTURY

Roger Sawtell
Northampton August 2008

Co-operative cartoon   2008

APPENDIX II   THE CO-OPERATIVE PRINCIPLES

Principles for the co-operative movement were originally established by the Rochdale Pioneers in the 19th. century. Without changing the fundamental issues, they have been revised from time to time by the International Co-operative Alliance (ICA), in the light of changing circumstances.

1 Voluntary and Open Membership
2 Democratic Member Control
3 Member Economic Participation
4 Autonomy and Independence
5 Education, Training and Information
6 Co-operation among Co-operatives
7 Concern for Community

Voluntary and Open Membership. Membership of the co-operative is open to all users willing to accept the responsibility, without gender, social, racial, political or religious discrimination.

Democratic Member Control. Equity share companies operate on a one-share-one-vote principle with the result that the company is dominated by large shareholders. In contrast, co-operative members have equal voting rights, one-member-one-vote (OMOV) similar to parliamentary democracy.

Member Economic Participation. Members receive benefits including the contemporary equivalent of the traditional co-op divi, in proportion to their transactions with the co-operative.

Autonomy and Independence. Co-operatives raise working capital on terms that ensure that control remains with the members and not with 'outside' investors.

Education, Training and Information. Co-operatives provide specific training and education for their members and inform the general public about the benefits of the co-operative concept of ownership and management.

Co-operation among Co-operatives. Co-operatives need to compete with other non-co-operative organisations in a mixed economy, but they also work together, locally and nationally, to strengthen the co-operative movement. For example, mutual building societies may merge or amalgamate but do not go bankrupt; no member has lost money in a mutual building society since 1945 and probably earlier.

Concern for Community. Co-operatives work for the sustainable development of the communities in which they operate.

rds   July 2009

APPENDIX III PEOPLE BEFORE PROFIT.
The Co-operative Movement

In the aftermath of the appalling financial crisis of 2007/8, the conventional business model of a bank or company owned by remote shareholders, is seen to be inadequate.   It is geared towards the benefit of its senior executives and its owners, resulting in huge salaries and   devious short-term concern for dividends and share prices.

Therefore the search is on for a viable alternative model, able to survive in the market place of a mixed economy but with social objects over and above the necessary financial ones.

The co-operative movement provides this alternative, especially for small businesses, owned and controlled by the working group. There are over 700,000 small businesses in UK (2016) and the co-operative structure is appropriate for many of them.

In the 19th century Christians were pioneers of more universal health care and education and it follows that, in this century, faith communities may well be the pioneers of new employee-owned co-operative businesses.   Daily Bread Co-operative, initiated in 1976 by a group from a local church congregation, is a model which others may replicate. However, co-operative businesses are by no means confined to faith communities; the common bond is that the working members wish to develop a business with objects beyond 'the bottom line' of maximising profit.

Daily Bread Co-operative started trading in 1980 and is now a group of about 25 people, mixing, packing and selling a wide range of wholefood products. Sales are £$1\frac{1}{2}$ million. As much as possible is Fairtrade and organic.

It is a registered society (21612R) under the Co-operative and Community Benefit Societies Act 2014 (which has replaced and consolidated the Industrial & Provident Societies Act 1965 (IPSA)) and is therefore part of the UK co-operative movement, subscribing to the seven Co-operative Principles. The Rules are the legal constitution of the business; they are on one sheet of paper and have not been changed since registration in 1976.

Decisions are taken at a weekly meeting of working members. There is no other decision-making body. Morning prayers in working time have been agreed procedure for over 30 years. It is estimated that 40,000 working hours have been 'lost' or 'gained' over this period.

Salaries are modest and related to needs rather than job title.
All working members are paid more than the national minimum wage. Work is provided for some disadvantaged people, especially those recovering from mental illness, irrespective of age or creed.

There are no outstanding loans or overdraft. The enterprise remains small and resists temptations to grow much larger or to open subsidiary branches. Lots of help is given to other co-operatives, by staff exchange for experience, loans for working capital, and advice when requested.

There is an understanding that there will be no redundancy. If trade diminishes, members will act together to keep the business going.

Daily Bread Co-operative,   The Old Laundry, Bedford Road, Northampton NN4 7AD   t: 01604 621531   f: 01604 603725
www.dailybread.co.uk   e: northampton@dailybread.co.uk
   on-line shop: www.ecofair.co.uk

APPENDIX IV   SWIMMING

I find it hard to explain the attraction of swimming but it is a fact that, whenever I am near water more than a few feet deep, I have the urge to jump in. This has led me into potential trouble such as being swept along a turbulent mill stream in rural France, and losing all sensation in fingers and toes after a very quick plunge into icy water off the San Juan islands in Puget Sound when visiting our son Peter in Seattle. The attraction is something to do with the pleasant feeling of being surrounded by a substance different from air. Water is supportive in a way that air is not and therefore one's body feels lifted and lighter. This feeling of wellbeing may be sufficient argument for open water bathing whether one swims or just stays immersed and static. For example, when plunging into the warmth of the Indian Ocean near Mumbai, my Indian friend insisted that it was a spiritual experience. He swam very slowly, hardly moving over the sea bed, and convinced me that it could be a time of meditation.   I have tried to follow this up at our local swimming pool, with limited success, as it is rather more crowded than the Indian Ocean. "*So sorry to get in your way, I was just contemplating the infinite.*"

When a problem arises at my desk I may put it on hold until I am in the pool and sometimes this helps to resolve it. Swimming is also an opportunity for intercessory prayer or for learning poetry but I find the poetry disappears again unless I repeat it several times a week. I have also found that it possible to 'sing' in one's head without making any sound and realise that singers can learn their music while sitting in a boring meeting or eating in a crowded restaurant or when swimming.   Next time I see someone eating alone I might ask him if he is rehearsing Don Giovanni.

Wherever I go I hope to find water and have swum on each side of the Atlantic, Pacific and Indian Oceans, and also in the 'Med, the Red and the Dead' as well as numerous other seas, lakes and rivers.

Among the less-frequented small Greek islands there is wonderful swimming from remote beaches and I have swum in places where possibly no one has ever swum before because the rocks are so sharp that it is nearly impossible to get in and out without cuts and scrapes.

For a time I declined to swim in chlorine-infested swimming pools but when I developed some back trouble I was advised to swim regularly and the sea was too far from Northampton and too cold for most of the year. I had a friend who used to potter down to a local urban lake late at night when the the park wardens were long gone home, but the bottom was very muddy and there was blue/green algae to contend with, so I swallowed my pride thirty years ago and have been a regular pool swimmer ever since.

We are a very different breed from the open water swimmers; some are content to meander up and down the pool but others come equipped with stop watches, streamlined goggles, tumble turns and energy drinks. For them it is totally for physical exercise and '*don't you dare get in my way*'. I find myself between the two and admit to being an obsessive recorder of figures since 1982. On a 'bad day' when there is heavy traffic in the pool it takes me 36 minutes to swim forty lengths, which is one kilometre, but with a lane to myself I can sometimes do it in 34 minutes. This is about average as I am faster than the meanderers but significantly slower than the folk with their energy drinks. My friend John, who swam for the Army team, told me his standard time was 23 minutes or less for a mile which is twice my speed. Recently(2016) I swam 100 lengths ($2\frac{1}{2}$ km./1.6 miles) but it took me 90 minutes. Despite trying to improve my technique, mostly about getting the breathing right, I get a little slower year by year and will probably come to a full stop in due course.

In some ways my fascination with swimming is strange because as a boy of about ten, a hesitant swimmer, I was serially 'ducked' by an older boy who did not realise I was gasping for breath. I felt I was drowning and it was an unforgettable horrible experience which re-occurred in dreams for years afterwards. We made sure our own children had swimming lessons and it is a special joy to see our grandchildren swimming more smoothly and faster than I ever could.

In 2007 when I turned eighty, I set myself the target of swimming 100 miles during the year. Two miles a week is not a lot to swim but every time I missed a week due to other activities or reluctance to walk to the pool in bad weather, it was a struggle to catch up. Since 2008 it has been downhill, or should it be downstream, all the way and in 2015 I only managed 60 miles.

My total mileage in 33 years from 1982 to 2015 is 2479 so if I had started from South Bridge, here in Northampton, swum down the River Nene into the North Sea, then turned south through the English Channel and across the Bay of Biscay to Gibraltar and into the Mediterranean, I would be well past Majorca by now. Unlike most sports, it is possible to continue swimming irrespective of age and, on a good day, I can still do 100 lengths which is 1.6 miles (2½ km.). In due course, I might even get as far as Greece.

APPENDIX V   WALKING

Sometimes with friends, often with Susan, with children and grandchildren, sometimes alone, walking has been a significant part of my life story, especially walking in wild country and among hills and by the sea. Family walks as a child were followed by exploration of the Yorkshire moors as a young man when I returned to Sheffield to work at Spear & Jackson. This, in turn, led to rock climbing on the gritstone edges and I have a photo of a climbing day in the company of John Hunt a year or two after he had led the first successful Everest expedition in 1953. This was before the advent of Vibram soles and we spent much time hammering nails into our leather walking boots to make them less slippery, and tricounis on the edges for rock climbing. To-day it seems laughable but it was all we could do in the 1950's.

As confidence increased I spent several holidays in the Alps, with friends, usually driving a 1950's Morris Minor and camping wild. Hung about with crampons and ice axes, Derek Grayson and I made an ascent of Cevedale 3768 m.(12,365'), the second highest peak in Italy. We think we reached the summit – there was a cairn – but visibility was down to a few metres and it was snowing. We saw no one else all day on the mountain and were glad to get down again to the lovely alpine meadows with marmots buzzing about, and to the equally lovely young Italian woman who was the warden of the rifugio. Derek ogled her hopefully but we got the impression that her love was far away. However, she did cook supper for us.

I have counted 35 countries visited over the years and have walked in the hill country of five continents. In New Zealand, Susan and I spent some days trekking in the hills of South Island and between jobs in 1974, Peter, aged 10, and I went trekking in Nepal and reached an altitude of about 5000m. (16,000') on the then unclimbed Langtang peak before deep snow and breathlessness made us turn back. Much later, visiting Peter in Seattle enabled us to spend a weekend with him in the Cascades where there are enough snow peaks, glaciers and trails to fill a lifetime. Then in Eritrea where the capital, Asmara, is at 2325 metres (7626') I was taken to the northern mountains where the freedom fighters had held out against the vastly more numerous Ethiopean army in the 1980's struggle for independence.

In 1993 Susan and I decided to explore some of the Greek islands and boarded a ferry to its ultimate destination, Astipalia. The traditional procedure for docking is for a seaman to hurl what looks like a tennis ball, with a light line attached, on to the quay where the local harbour master gathers in the line which is also attached to the ferry's heavy-duty mooring cable. He loops the the cable round a bollard on the quay and the ferry can then winch itself up to the landing stage. This usually happens quickly and smoothly but it depends on the harbour master or his mate being ready on the quay. On this, our first experience of island-hopping, when we reached an unknown island the captain announced that we could go no further because the harbour master, receiver of the tennis ball, on Astipalia was on strike ! There was no other way of landing passengers there so we had to disembark at Amorgos, fell in love with the island and have returned there over twenty times, often with friends and family. We like the people, the swimming and the food.

It is a mountainous place and the walking is superb. We know just about every track and every difficult-to-access beach on the island. Visitors sometimes underestimate the hazards and some years ago a party of French people found their way down a cliff to a distant beach but could not climb back. They phoned the police who showed little concern and referred them to a western European resident who knew the island well. He offered to bring them out for €80 which they refused. Eventually a local man agreed to rescue them without charge and, with the help of his donkey, he escorted them back to his taverna where they chose not to stay for a meal. Maybe they were broke but it rightly upset the islanders that their willing help had not been more appreciated.

We have been told numerous stories of happenings on this wonderful island and were unsurprised to learn that they had been very hospitable in 2015 to refugees from Syria arriving unexpectedly on a remote beach. Amorgos has become steadily more popular for walkers over the last twenty years, but it has not been overrun by visitors because the winds and ferries are not sufficiently reliable. On one occasion we had to wait three days for the ferry to come.

Like most Greek islands, Amorgos has many churches, some in isolated places. The one to which we have become most attached is a small uninhabited monastery on a lofty cliff top looking towards Jerusalem 1000 km. to the east, with no land intervening. In 1993 it was in very poor condition, full of rubble and visited mainly by goats, but over the ensuing twenty years it has been gradually restored by the family of our friend Giorgis who acts as caretaker and keeps his bees nearby. At the summer festival, local people and visitors come from all over the island to attend the lengthy Greek Orthodox service and also to enjoy Giorgis' honey and his goat stew. The island people have welcomed us year by year and we, in turn, have introduced several friends to this place so special to us. If it was more accessible I might ask for my ashes to be scattered there but I must accept that our local nature reserve is a more realistic option. There was talk of making a road to Theologos but I hope it will not happen because the pilgrimage walk up the donkey track from the village is part of the experience.

A different and longer pilgrim walk was on the Camino du Nord in Spain with Michael and Anne Jones in 2002. We crossed the Pyrenees and walked south for ten days, stopping to sing Taizé chants and visit innumerable churches. I think Michael was the only person in the rifugio dormitories to change into pyjamas every night and Anne dried her pants by flying them from her rucksack as the day warmed up. Standards must be maintained.

Visiting India with colleagues to discuss employee-ownership with Gandhians I never got to the hills, but made another memorable pada-yatra (pilgrimage walk) from village to village, accepting simple hospitality and holding impromptu meetings every evening with the local elders. Vinoba Bhave, highly respected disciple of Gandhi, had walked for seven years visiting hundreds of villages. He welcomed us to his ashram and I asked him what we western Europeans could do to help India. He said, "*Be vegetarians. If crops are for cows there is not enough food for people. If cows are not for eating, the world can be fed.*" I have been a vegetarian ever since.

As the consumer market has responded to the appeal of country walking in UK, new ideas for special 'walking socks' have appeared year by year.

There were 'self-wicking ' socks, whatever that means, and then '1000 mile' socks, guaranteed to last out the distance. Mine were in holes after 300 miles and the shop reluctantly returned the money which was sufficient to buy five pairs of 'ordinary' socks. Then I tried 'double-layer' socks but one layer shrunk more than the other in the wash, causing uncomfortable wrinkles. In Scotland we put plastic bags over our socks to keep dry before Gore-tex became commonplace.

Recently, being retired and having the time, I go walking most days, often just to do the shopping or going to the swimming pool. In 2007 aged 80, keeping a mileage record for the 1000-mile socks gave me the idea of aiming to walk 1000 miles in a year. This appealed to my obsessive concern for measuring times and distances. At first sight, this is not a strenuous objective as it can be achieved by walking an hour a day, but other happenings such as travelling or illness or bad weather play havoc with this average so I found that it was necessary to walk for at least 1½ hours on every 'walking' day to make up for the 'non-walking' days. Here are the figures from my diaries :-

2007	walk	648.5 miles	swim	90.9 miles
2008	"	1023.5 "	"	100.1 "
2009	"	963.0 "	"	84.5 "
2010	"	951.5 "	"	58.5 "
2011	"	1053.5 "	"	71.9 "
2012	"	955.0 "	"	67.5 "
2013	"	886.0 "	"	73.7 "
2014	"	773.0 "	"	65.9 "

2008 was the only year in which I achieved the 'double' of 1000 miles walking and 100 miles swimming.

After 2014 I decided there were better priorities than this daily record keeping (but I still can't resist noting swimming distances).   Our GP, Dr. Kausar, says I am reaping the rewards for having always taken plenty of exercise.

The Grand Union canal is good for walkers as it avoids traffic and wanders through some surprisingly remote countryside between Northampton and London. In 2002 Susan and I walked 106 miles in eight stages from our house to the outflow into the Thames at Limehouse, East London. I repeated this in 2008 as a sponsored walk for Christian Aid and raised nearly £1,000.

Walking is, of course, the best way to observe what is happening in the world whether it is the ever-changing life of the trees or the ever-changing habits of the people around us.
Both Susan and I have adopted the habit to talking to strangers on the path or in the street and at the checkout and have learned a lot in so doing. The annual mileage we do in the car is diminishing year by year but, hopefully, we can both keep on walking.

Bench installed at Pitsford Water Nature Reserve. 2010

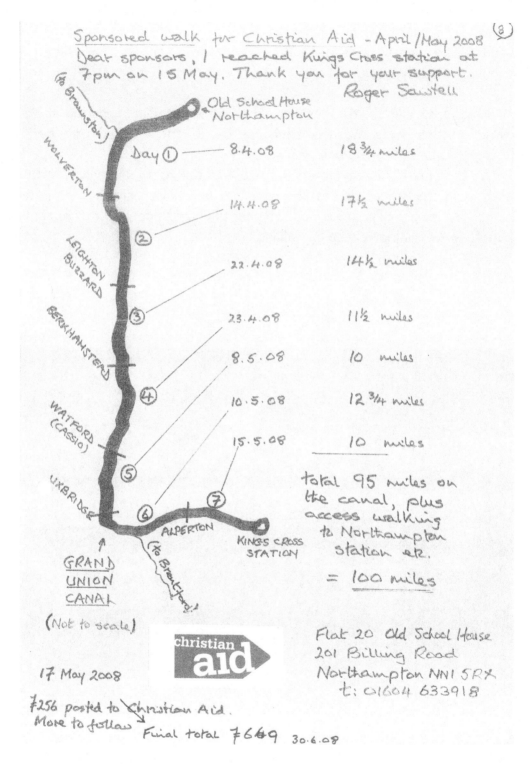

Sponsored walk for Christian Aid - April/May 2008   (8)
Dear sponsors, I reached Kings Cross station at
7pm on 15 May. Thank you for your support.
                                Roger Sawtell

Old School House
Northampton

Day ① ——— 8.4.08   18¾ miles

14.4.08   17½ miles

②

22.4.08   14½ miles

③

23.4.08   11½ miles

8.5.08   10 miles

④

10.5.08   12¾ miles

15.5.08   10 miles

⑤

⑦

⑥

ALPERTON   KINGS CROSS
                STATION

total 95 miles on
the canal, plus
access walking
to Northampton
station etc.

= 100 miles

GRAND
UNION
CANAL

(Not to scale)

17 May 2008

£256 posted to Christian Aid.
More to follow   Final total £669 30.6.08

Flat 20 Old School House
201 Billing Road
Northampton NN1 5RX
t: 01604 633918

christian aid

Northampton to London- sponsored walk for Christian Aid

APPENDIXA VI SHARING BREAD AND WINE – reclaiming the concept of agape (reprinted from *Celebrating 10 Years of Prayer in To-day's World* - Emmaus House of Prayer 2014)

There are innumerable Bible references to eating together and being hospitable. In the very early days, Abraham, sitting by his tent at Mamre, says to three unknown visitors, ' Let me bring a little bread ' *(Genesis 18:5 NRSV)*. In the New Testament there are three Gospel passages which describe the bread and wine ceremony initiated by Jesus, which we now variously describe as the Lord's Supper, Holy Communion, Mass, Eucharist, Agape *(Matthew 26:26-30, Mark 14:22-25, Luke 22:14-20)*.

The Mennonite scholar, Eleanor Kreider has written extensively on the Lord's Supper (*Communion Shapes Character,* Herald Press 1997). Her historical survey of the practices of early Christians indicates they met as small groups during the week for agape evening meals and then a larger gathering for eucharist on Sunday. Both were sacramental occasions with bread and wine.

As the Gospel spread, churches were built which were designed for corporate worship, usually without facilities for eating together. Mission was mainly westwards to Europe where the climate was colder and doors kept closed, so neighbourly fellowship was more difficult to retain. These buildings had advantages for preaching and teaching but the small group 'table fellowship' of the agape gradually faded out of the liturgy.
The fundamentals of the agape in the Early Church were :-

A meal during which the participants give bread and wine to each other, in the manner of the Gospel narratives, together with prayers and Bible reading;

The bread was baked in the household where it was to be eaten and wine was the normal drink of the time, made from grapes grown in local vineyards;

The leader might be any of the people present, not necessarily an ordained minister.

With respect to the wine, Jesus' words, 'drink ye all of it' *(Matthew 26-27 AV)*, can infer that the wine should be consumed in its entirety and none left in the cup. However, the New Revised Standard Version (NRSV), widely regarded as the most accurate translation of the earliest manuscripts now available to scholars, gives ' drink from it, all of you ' and the Jerusalem Bible has 'drink all of you from this'. Although some take a different view, the majority of scholars now appear to think Jesus' words imply that he intended everyone round the table, without reference to age or church membership, to be invited to join in the giving and taking of the bread and wine.

Some would say such inclusivity is even more important for visitors and children because it is a practical example of the love of God extended to all, rather than only to believers. There is a poignant incident in Marilynne Robinson's novel *Gilead* (Virago Press 2005) in which the young wife of John Ames, an elderly retired Protestant minister, suggests he gives this bread to their son, aged seven. She takes it for granted that the bread, representing the body of Christ, should be available to all present and not confined to an inner circle. With transparent simplicity she says, 'You should give him some of that' and the minister realises that she goes straight to the heart of the matter, without the complications of academic theology or practice.

Today a few churches, including Mennonites, have continued with table fellowship. Others on the fringes see the merit of agape, and various liturgies are in circulation. From personal experience, the proceedings of the Neighbours Community, a residential Christian community of households in Northampton from 1984 to 2007, record numerous agape occasions, some spontaneous and others planned in advance. In addition to community members, usually there would be visitors present and sometimes children.

Another example of the significance of eating together is the Elders whose remit is the spiritual health of Quaker meetings. Quakers hold that all life is sacramental and therefore they do not have specific sacramental liturgies such as eucharist or agape. The Elders of Northampton Meeting recently decided to change the procedure for their small group meetings to include a shared meal in each other's homes. This changed the focus of their discussions.

 When Jesus was at Emmaus, after the resurrection, it was in the breaking of bread that the two disciples recognised him (Luke 24:31). Let us pray that we may also recognise Jesus in the breaking of bread and the sharing of food. Perhaps we should reclaim the concept of agape, eating together in a reverential and prayerful manner as a vital part of our lifestyle as followers of Jesus? These reflections need consideration in more depth. It is not my intention to decry current Eucharistic practices which are clearly an important part of the spiritual life of countless Christians and, if I am drawn towards what may be a controversial position of more 'open communion', then I pray to do so in a spirit of charity rather than a spirit of criticism of those who take a less inclusive view.   Roger Sawtell 2014

APPENDIX VII   AN AGAPE LITURGY

The person leading the worship welcomes guests and outlines the liturgy. Songs may be sung.
Reading. Matthew 26:26-28 NRSV : While they were eating, Jesus took a loaf of bread, and after blessing it he broke it, gave it to the disciples and said, "Take, eat, this is my body." Then he took a cup, and after giving thanks he gave it to them, saying, " Drink from it, all of you; for this is my blood of the new covenant, which is poured out for many for the forgiveness of sins."

Leader (holding the bread): This bread, made from grains and seeds, risen with yeast, is the bread which is broken as sometimes we feel broken, wounded, defeated by circumstances. This is 'bread', a symbol of our prosperity which is not so much of our making but often due to happenstance and by grace, the unmerited favour of a loving God. This is the bread which is also a symbol of our life together, committed to nourish each other. Creator God, we remember those who are hungry. Your people cry out for justice. We ask for strength to put our prosperity to the service of the poor and disadvantaged.
All: Your world is one world and we are stewards of it.

Leader: This is the bread, given for us, which Jesus tells us to eat together to remind us of his life and death on this earth. Let us eat this bread in silence.

> *Each person takes a piece of bread and gives it to his/her neighbour,then hands on the plate.   Grace may be said.*
> *Then food is brought in and the meal is eaten*

After the meal: Leader (holding the cup): This is the wine which Jesus told us to share, in remembrance of him, and to be aware of our need for forgiveness. As we drink from this cup, let us forgive one another and all who seek our forgiveness.
> *The cup is passed round for each person to drink, in silence*

All: The grace of our Lord Jesus Christ, the love of God and the fellowship of the Holy Spirit be with us all evermore. Amen.

APPENDIX VIII   PUBLICATIONS

Sharing Our Industrial Future – a study of employee participation
(The Industrial Society 1968)

Industrial Co-operatives – A Guide to the ICOM Model Rules
(Industrial Common Ownership Movement 1977
  2nd. Edition, with Michael Campbell   1980)

A Simple Communion – arranged for house groups
(Disciples Press 1978)

How to Convert a Company into an Industrial Co-operative
(Co-operative Development Agency   1979)

The Church That Meets In Your House
(Daily Bread Co-operative 1980)

Blueprint for 50 Co-operatives
(Co-operative Development Agency   1985)

*(editor) The Call to Mission Answered – Ted Wickham and the Sheffield
Industrial Mission 1944-1959 By Philip Bloy (Disciples Press   2000)*

Reflections from a Long Marriage   -   with Susan Sawtell
Swarthmore Lecture 2006   (Quaker Books 2006)

*Employee-Owned Co-operative Businesses in Northamptonshire 1850-
2010*   (Daily Bread Co-operative 2010)

*The Man Who Brought Light – the story of Edward Leslie who initiated a
remarkable social and technical development in northwest Scotland.*
(FastPrint Publishing   2011)

Under One Roof – the story of a Christian community.
(Darton Longman & Todd 2015

APPENDIX IX   Curriculum Vitae

1924	My parents. Horace Sawtell (known as David) married Barbara Leslie at St. James, Piccadilly, London.
1925	My brother David born
1927	**June 19. Born at 187 Rustlings Road, Sheffield**
1931	My sister Nancy born
1931	Moved to Oak Cottage, Alderley Edge, Cheshire
1935-41	Arnold House School, Llandulas, North Wales
1941-45	Bedford School, Bedford
1939	Moved to 184 Tom Lane, Sheffield
	Moved to The Farm, Wortley, near Sheffield
1945-48	Clare College, Cambridge. State Bursary.
1948	BA. Mechanical Sciences Tripos.
1948-50	English Electric Ltd., Rugby. Graduate Apprentice
1950-66	Spear & Jackson Ltd. Sheffield.
1957	September 14. Married to Susan Mary Flint by Canon Ted Wickham (Sheffield Industrial Mission), assisted by Rev. Raymond Bailey (Iona Community). Moved to 15 Sale Hill, Sheffield
1958-64	Our children born. Ruth (1958), Mary (1960), Rebecca (1963), Peter (1964)
1961	Freeman - The Company of the Cutlers of Hallamshire
1962	Justice of the Peace - Sheffield
1966	Clare College. Sabbatical term
1967	Journey to Jerusalem
1968	*Sharing Our Industrial Future* published
	Trylon Ltd. Wollaston, Northants.
	Moved to 24 Weston Way, Northampton
1974-80	Self-employed. ICOM/ ICOF.
	Industrial Common Ownership Act (1976)
1978-81	Board Member – Co-operative Development Agency
1980-95	Daily Bread Co-operative Ltd., Northampton.
1984	Moved to 146 Ardington Road, Northampton.
1984-2007	The Neighbours Community 140–148 Ardington Rd.
1986	Chairman of Trustees – Traidcraft Ltd. Gateshead
1991	Travelled round the world, visiting friends.
2006	Swarthmore Lecture, Religious Society of Friends,
2007	Moved to 20 Old School House, Northampton.
2015	Darton Longman & Todd published *Under One Roof*

Printed in Great Britain
by Amazon

27811522R00112